Branded &Bold

A mentor guided journey of discovery to your true identity and strategically asserting yourself into your ultimate life role.

Curtis L. Walker

Copyright © 2018

All rights reserved. No part of this book may be reproduced, stored in retrieval systems, or transmitted in any form, or by any means, electronic, mechanical, photocopying, recording or otherwise, without written permission except I the case of brief quotations embodied in critical articles and reviews.

ISBN: 9780997-1166816

DEDICATION

This is dedicated to the mentors and heroes that took the time to invest in me and encouraged me to pass it on. Together, we will shape the world.

TABLE OF CONTENTS

ACKNOWLEDGMENTS i

Introduction 1

Week 1 – The Dream 20

Day 1 - Peaceful bliss 29

Day 2 - Another Reality... 33

Day 3 - Soul Food 37

Day 4 - Beyond Beliefs 42

Day 5 - Problems solved 46

Day 6 - Worth Pursuing 51

Day 7 – Rejoice in it 55

Week 2 – The Awakening 61

Day 8 - Crush the Contract 64

Day 9 - Dare to be different.. 69

Day 10 - No Apologies 73

Day 11 - What's calling you?....................................... 78

Day 12 - Turn the page 83

Day 13 - Wake up determined… 87

Day 14 - Inviting Vision 92

Week 3 – Arise 97

Day 15 - Drop weight 100

Day 16 - Take a new path 105

Day 17 - Get Up! 109

Day 18 - Better than Yesterday 113
Day 19 - Time to Develop 118
Day 20 - This is Going to Hurt 122
Day 21 - Response-Able 126
Week 4 – Get Ready 131
Day 22 - What is it, really? 134
Day 23 - Load up! 139
Day 24 - Choose the challenge 143
Day 25 - Limiting Limits 147
Day 26 - Transform from the inside out 151
Day 27 - Greater growth 155
Day 28 - If you Need It… 159
Week 5 – Get Set 163
Day 29 - Where is your focus? 166
Day 30 - Chunk it! 171
Day 31 - Overcome Obstacles 175
Day 32 - Refuse to bow 180
Day 33 - Fight the enemy within 185
Day 34 – Ready the resources 189
Day 35 – Grounded 193
Week 6 – Go! 197
Day 36 - A Traveled Road 200
Day 37 - Soul on fire 204
Day 38 - Climb! 208

Day 39 - Reach!... 212
Day 40 - Grow!.. 216
Day 41 - Reach for the heavens.................................. 221
Day 42 - Lift up! 225
Conclusion 229
Prolog... 233
About the Author: 237

ACKNOWLEDGMENTS

I want to give thanks to the people that I have come to know as friend. There are too many to name but they once were clients, but now I call them friends and peers. You have worked with me and learned from my teachings, and you have acted as my teacher and pushed me to new levels. It was your work and push that encouraged me to write about what we have worked through.

I also want to give thanks to my wife, Tami. She is my enabler. She clears the path so I can go out and reach people. She fights to make sure my distractions are addressed and sets the environment so I can focus and develop.

My thanks go out to the team of designers, editors, and publishers that put in the work to make this book possible. Thanks for sticking with me.

Now let's go get it done!!

INTRODUCTION

Identity Crisis:

There were days when I struggled being me. I felt lost and confused about who I was and the role in life that I was to play. I questioned my existence. I questioned my beginning. "Why?" was the question continually on my lips.

My name is Curtis Walker, and this is my journey and story. Branded and Bold was birthed out of a ton of questions that I had. It was birthed out of challenges that I faced and discoveries that I go to make. It comes from people that I met along my life's journey. Success and failures. It was brought forth from my moments of brokenness and embarrassment.

Why Branded and Bold?

Well, to be honest, it's catchy. The name of this book rolls off the tongue quite easily. Also, it comes right out and states what it means and invites so many questions. At the heart of this book, it addresses your identity and the way you choose to manage it, and it gets up in your face and demands you to make some bold declarations to what you can and will do from this time forward. Your identity is not a thing to be taken lightly. It's like the name you were given at birth. Each name carries a meaning, and many of us know that, and we work at fulfilling some resemblance to that meaning. However, the bulk of us functions on autopilot. Just chilling and going with the flow. We have let life beat and quiet us down while locking on a submission hold. Well, I am here to coach you. Just like in a good wrestling match, when the odds are against you, and it feels like you are about to lose, all it takes is some minor tweaking from a good coach that could make all the difference.

So, let me start off by making a bold declaration. If you choose to go any further with this book and pursue this journey, I will help you understand the shaping process of your identity and encourage you to live through these 6 bold declarations.

6 Bold Declarations:

1. **DREAM:** I will accept my divine **DREAM** without limits and seek every way possible to move them into reality.
2. **AWAKE:** I will **AWAKEN** to my true calling and pursue it with relentless passion
3. **ARISE:** I will **ARISE** and engage life at its highest level.
4. **READY:** I will make myself **READY** for challenges, knows and unknown through resources I collect.
5. **SET:** I will **SET** my focus, plan, and commitment and will only settle for success.
6. **GO:** I will **GO** and set this world on fire with my unlimited being and transform its future.

As I was challenged to write this or even to come up with a title for this project, you will discover that what you are being guided through were excerpts from my personal journals. I edited much of it and toned it down so that the heart of it could resonate with you. Over the past 8 years, I have been on a deep journey of self-discovery. I not only had to come to terms with my own personal identity I had to lean the power of thought and personal contacts. We will get deeper into what that means as we move forward, but let me lay down my contract. Once I lay it out, I am responsible for bringing this into the universe.

My contract:

I will get this finished work and all of its expanded development into the hands of people around the globe and encourage them to discover their identity and calling and take ownership of shaping their destiny with a high sense of responsibility. I will encourage my readers to engage in mentorship at the heights level. I am committed to instituting a distribution platform that will get this program in the hands of 6 MILLION people within 6 years (By December 31, 2023) by any means necessary.

How bold is that!?!?

Do we need another book?

This is not just another book. It is another story. Everyone has a story. It is a story of transition and hope. There can never be enough stories of encouragement, hope, perseverance and the advancement of mankind. It's becomes too common placed to editorialize life down to a summary and drape it in darkness and disperse for the sake of financed sponsorship. This book pushes and pulls, and it digs deep and elevates. It is challenging. It was challenging for me to write it. It would not let me marginalize its conception or delivery. It demanded to be written and re-written. This is more than a book; it's a movement. It came from my heart, but it was inspired at a higher level than I and the Initiator insist that it gets delivered and dispersed to the world. This is not a book but its soon to be an experience.

Who is Curtis Walker?

Blessed and born in the city of Pontiac Michigan in 1965 and I had the pleasure and privilege of being born to the hardest working people I have ever known. James and Jessie Walker. My mom and dad moved from Alabama to Michigan in the late 50s. They may have moved out of the south, but the south would never move out of them. They passed down wisdom, love, and heritage. There were no dull moments in or around my home. I had five sisters and one older brother. I was youngest. The last of the greatest. (I say that just in case my sister's ever read this. Just wanted to remind them of that fact.)

My family had limited income and many expenses with all the mouths to feed. There were high expectations for everyone. We all had to do our part in order for our family unit to function. However, me being the youngest, I had trouble fitting in. There was a huge age gap between my youngest sister and myself. So, early on, I felt confused. There were times when I felt like I had not just one mother, but six. It was challenging, to say the least.

I was born and raised in the north, but I raised with a southern heritage. If you ever get a chance to spend time talking to me, you would hear a hint of a southern draw in my expression. I am acquainted with the ways of the south. I have roots that enable me to thrive and survive in both settings. Respect, honor, and obedience was the order of the day. You did what you were told, and you didn't ask. Much of that rearing established the foundation in how I operated in my little world.

When I was 17, I joined the U.S. Marines. Day one, I had my identity stripped from me along with my emotions and will. I was no longer an individual with a personality. I became a working, functioning member of a unit. I became one with the Corp. Once again I followed orders and towed the line. I had my days, months, years of my life ordered and planned out. I served nine years in the reserves.

Along with the Marines, I served and supported many companies. I worked as an IT contractors for General Motors, Ford, and Chrysler. I developed as an IT professional. In my later career, I moved from automotive to the banking industry. Overall I have been doing IT work for 30 years. One of my greatest discoveries of all the things that I have done with my career is that I absolutely despise working on computers (Other than to write this book). The other truth that I discovered was I absolutely love people.

Some who have heard me speak would say that I am a motivational speaker. However, my real passion is to help people discover and move closer to their motives. I help them find their "Why?" then I push them to deeper questions that map out their "WHAT?" and "HOW?" During my first half century, I learned how to toe the line and stay in step with what was going on around me. I got good at it, but I never felt complete or fulfilled. My drive and passion were not in what I was actively doing. One of the things I advise my clients is if at any times you found yourself not happy and fulfilled, check your plan and how you're working on it. If your heart is telling you to do something that you are not actively working on, then your betrayed heart will never let you experience happiness. Once you discover that something is out of sync, then you owe it to your sprite to take rapid change.

I've allowed my mind, body, and spirit to now get on the same page. I examined who was at the helm of my life, and I, with respect and conviction, thanked them for their help, support, and leadership up until now, and then I took the wheel. I moved to a position of responsibility, and now I am on my fantastic adventure. I'm doing some things that I love, and I am feeling fulfilled. I see the benefit of this experience, and I am committed to aiding others on their journey of self-actualization and strategically asserting themselves into their true rooted out calling.

When I started this writing project, I was going to do a deep dive study of Life-Branding and hit you all with some fancy jargon and try to dazzle you with graphs and charts to show you how smart I was and to impress you with my research. But as I got deeper into this project, I had to come to the point of realness with myself and commit to my truest expression. You see, my life has been moving along this fantastic journey, and I have been blessed by so many people that have encouraged and shaped my development. So, I wanted to share my heart and give you a glimpse of my journey.

This training is life-coach centered, and you will find that much of this is structured to produce some good results as you progress through the chapters and daily work, but it is designed to work as a deeper guide in a life coaching session, or in a group structure life coaching session. Overall, it is not a book to read or an audio to consume, but this is challenging to move you to action. I hate wasting people's time by just moving the air around. When I work with my coaching clients, they expect results from my time, and in honor of that relationship, I place some tough demands on them. So, let me be honest and fair. If you are going to pick this up, I expect you to either stop now, put this back on the shelf and walk away, if you are not going to do the work. But if you are bold and brave enough to do something about your destiny, then let's get ready to work. I mean we go deep, and roll up our sleeves, and get ready to gut it out, sweat and maybe even cry as we get ready to run this race.

I am as clear as I can, about this matter. This is a race! At this time. I am in training to run a half marathon. 13.1 miles. For me, this is no joke. Much of the principles in this book is related to managing one's own life brand, but it also about how to –re-brand yourself. You see, to look at my health condition it doesn't seem likely that I would be able to make this run by July of 2018. But you see, this is a **DREAM** that has been pursuing me. The last doctor's report moved me to be more **AWAKE**. I have chosen to **ARISE** and take ownership of my health. I and **READYing** myself for this challenging journey. I have **SET** goals for myself, and it is my passion that on race day, I will be able to **GO** with reckless abandonment.

No, I am not encouraging you to take up running, but I am encouraging you to take up **LIFE**. Your own life. I want you to get excited about what it looks like and feels to take ownership and manage the trajectory of where your life is heading. I want to you get excited about the strategies you use with how to place yourself in the marketplace. But not just limited there, I want you deeply think about your placement in time, history and the contribution that you have been called to make in this world.

You see, many I have talked to about this subject, have come to the conclusion that they have been running on maybe on 2 cylinders, at best, when they have another 6 to choose from. I want to offer a tune-up and increase performance. I don't want you just be in the race of life, but I want you in the winner's circle. I want you to leave it all on the track.

The World's Richest Place:

I have heard it said that the graveyard is the world's richest place. You see, there are those who have lived safe, moderate, and none challenged lives to the point that they have chosen comfort over growth. And I discover that growth comes with pain. People naturally do not want pain, so they will settle and even did long before they reach the grave. Yet, many started out as dreamers. Excited about the possibilities of life. Wanting to be this and that and desire to get out there and make a name for themselves. So, what happened to their dreams? The common and obvious pattern is that they placed their dreams in the hands of others and then they let them get crushed by the weight of the words of doubt. People when practiced living down to their own fears and choosing to conform to the calls of a tribe, spoke limitation to them, and persuaded to give up on foolishness for the sake of conformity and comfort. So, like many others that had gone before them toned down, and fell in line and give up. They chose to deprive the world of a cure to cancer, mean to come up with alternative fuel. Ways to end global hunger, active methods to break global poverty, so forth and so on. They simply let those dreams die with them and go to the grave.

It Stops today

But I say NO. I personally have chosen to change my tune and alter my life. First of all, I had to get real and count my blessings. My life has been tough, and I have had so many losses and set back, but I have also been abundantly blessed. I was born with a silver spoon in my mouth, and I was born to the right set of parents. We grow up with some of the best challenges being that we were an African American family that came from the south and both my mom and dad worked hard. I got the privilege to be raised with and by my 5 sisters and 1 brother. The 9 of us lived in a 3 bedroom house. We were tight! Close is a better word. I was blessed to be born black in this country in 1965. A time when the cultural landscape was shifting to higher possibilities. Both my parents had diabetes and heart disease, and it ended their lives early, but the life they lived, they both laid down some powerful roots and legacy like no other. They granted me values that still stand with me to today. They rose out of the atrocities of the 60's in the south. They held a strong attitude toward possibilities and prosperity through hard work. They passed that passion along to their children and grandchildren. It's the motor and fuel that drive me today. It's GPS that gives me the truth about my destiny and well as where I stand today. I'm in motion and my future in undeniably promising. I refuse to lose. I care to share. I am old, so I must mold. I shape my destiny as well as others that I get the privilege to interact with. So, as you get ready to get blessed and inspired, you are about to get your soil turned, and some seeds are about to get planted. The intent is for it to go deep and lay roots. For the ground it has landed, it will face some storms and set back along with floods and fires, but with no doubt, it is being tended. There is a high expectation of growth under some insurmountable obstacles. Yet, hope none the less. Growth will take place and harvest so vast that it will bless you now and for generations to come.

Are you with me? <u>Let's Go!</u>

More on why I called this book Branded and Bold?

Well, I wanted something catchy, or you would not have picked up this book. But there is a deeper meaning. I have spent over 30 years in the corporate world as well as in the military. I have learned what it is to work hard as well as smart. I have learned how to follow as well as lead. But, the saddest thing I have learned to do is to conform without purpose or choice. You see, much I did, as far as a career has been event-driven. I have done jobs that were either easy, or circumstances demanded I do. I spent so much time to do the work and to fit in so not to rock the boat; then I forgot that I was inside of me. I forgot that I had a dream. I forgot that I had a voice. At every turn, when my voice wanted to speak or ask questions, there was someone there trying to quiet me down and to tell me that I needed to be careful so not get in trouble. My motto today is to BE TROUBLE. I am intentional about being trouble for problems. My goal is to master conquering problems at the highest level. The first place I fight problems is internal. There are days when I am having my alone time, I get loud, bold and I have it out with myself. If you ever get the fortunate opportunity to witness it, you could swear that those moments are like a schizophrenic episode. There are times I will get in a mirror, and I have one of the hardest pep talks with myself. I call myself: CHAMPION, WARRIOR, and MASTER OF DESTINY. I get in my own face. I tell myself that "YOU OWN YOUR VOICE AND REFUSE TO BE SILENT." I tell myself that no one owns me. My destiny is calling, and I am obligated to answer. I let my sessions with myself build up the momentum that carries out to my external. In contrast, I spent too much of my beginning life conforming to events and shape of where people felt they should place me. But, I had to stop and ask WHY? Why is this acceptable? Slavery is over, and I have the power to make some choices. No matter where I was placed on this earth, I have the power of choice, and that gives me the power to change. There is no government nor spiritual mandate given to me nor can they take it away. I define my own meaning and interpretation of life's events, and I now pass that charge on to you. Will you dare to stand, not with me, but with yourself and for yourself? Will you let your internal voice become a sound and bold? Set a course that is purposeful, noble and true to you. Feel the wind in your sails. Weight anchor. Get on the track of life and take your mark. Feel the wind on your back. Whatever motivates you, use it, but by all means, GO!

What is Life-Brand Management?

You are labeled as something. From the day you were born, you are granted and gender, skin color, class, and prescribed a culture. Much of which was pre-selected for you. Some would say it was good or bad, prominent or small, humble or great. No matter what, it was given to you. But by grace, you grew, got older, and aware. You started to understand what choices were. You got to understand consequences. But, for the most part, you have been managed and handled. This in itself is not a bad thing. But if you have not stooped to ask WHY are you PERSONALLY, doing what you are doing, then you may be missing out on connecting with your greater fulfillment in life. Life is a gift and what we do with it is our gift to the world. You see, the world we live in was our original gift and we, all of its inhabitants, are its stewards. She has so many secrets locked inside. Some have been revealed, but there are so many more treasures that they need to discover. The issue is, we have been lulled to sleep into thinking that a lifelong conformity is a way to get the best out of life. That is a path with limitations. That path may serve if we are OK to stay within the slotted tracks. But like a balloon, once it is blow up, and inflated, it cannot shrink back into its same old shape. This training will stretch you into a new shape. I wanted to excite your appetite for the possibilities of life and things you could and really should do. Above all, I am promoting awareness and ownership of what is happening in your life right now. Review your habits and thoughts, and through that maturing process, you will be moved to a state of knowing and believing. You will know and believe that you can shape your future into being anything you want it to be. For many of you, that will be far-fetched as if someone told you that you would be making a trip to Mars. Years ago, travel to Mars was not a possibility either, but today, that is a reality that is coming very close. So, what I am saying to you, get serious about taking charge of your future? You owe it to yourself to explore this journey.

Don't Quit Your Day Job:

If you are in a career, this book is not about deciding to leave one's career for something better. But it's about becoming self-aware and mature enough to take account the success and doors that have been opened for you to get to where are currently, and to give thanks and grow from a position of gratitude in discovering how you can fill up your space and time with the purest and fullest essence of who you are. Be MORE in the moment. You will find by mastering your moments; then you can develop the leverage to shape your tomorrow in an effective manner. I consider everyone and everything to be my teacher about myself. If you are in a job, consider it free education. You are working for people or organization that you feel are not appreciating you, then don't do the typical, quitting to get something better. Get better in the tough circumstance and let your new found strength move you to where you are truly supposed to be. Become so aware, that you can map out a clear path to your true calling. And with a reason WHY, and a good map, then you can have the needed tools to navigate to where you are supposed to be. The WHERE may not be a place, but a state of mind.

WHO is this for?

When I started this journey, I was working with a group of small business owners, and this was designed to help them with the psychology required to branding themselves in the marketplace, but this past summer I got the grand opportunity to work with a bunch of college students, that opened my eyes to how this can greatly be applied to catapult them into the marketplace in a more effective way. So, this book is fitting for any individual who wants more out of life, which may be lacking directions. Someone who has not taken the time to ask the tough questions. Someone who is willing to go on a journey. Ultimately, someone with a passion to serve. You will see, no matter what you do or what industry you are in or even if you are a homemaker, we all have one thing in common. Serving our fellow man. This guild will help you to understand where you can best serve and to clearly define the value and how to serve as many as you can in your allotted time on this big blue ball.

Why do they need it?

Why ask why? Because we need to. It takes a brave, a mature person to take steps to ask themselves why do they do anything at all. It's easy to go through the motion, but life becomes more impactful and purposeful when we choose to ask why. So why is this book needed? Have you ever tried to navigate through woods without a map and a compass? Especially at night? I have. Not an easy task. I had to perform land navigation in the military. What I found is that a good soldier will know his terrain and acclimate himself to his surroundings and map out the best path to any given objective. To proceed without a plan or a map is asking for trouble. What I am offering is not a cut and dry map, but what I am going to do is to partner with you in the development of your own personal map. We are not all on the same journey, and we are not all headed to the same destination, but we all need a good methodology to root out what our own personal plan should look like.

What difference did it make in my life?

There are days where I felt like Pinocchio. Constructed by hand, given limited purpose, but yet there was some magical calling on my life for something more. I have been working in information technology field for the past 30 years. I have been working on computers before computers were commonly used. I have built, installed, supported, networked, developed and troubleshot many issues. But as of lately, I discovered, that something was lacking. My awakening was that I realized that I hated computers. But in addition to that, I found that I have a high love and passion for people and how they think and how to engineer success. So, within my self-discovery, I had to go to work on myself. Making deep discovery into who I was, and where I wanted to go. Digging deeper into my WHY. I found that I am a great storyteller and that I like to communicate life and business principles in story form that helps people quickly discover and move to a better place in life. I am committed to personal development, and I press to get better every day. I am passionate about taking what I have experienced over the years and as of late to the world. There are people I have impacted, and there is a hunger for more from me. I am committed to record all that I can in writing, audio and video form so that they can share it on a broad platform. I feel happier and free. Not just for the future, but I'm genuinely happy right now. I am excited about this moment, and I am grateful for all that has happened and how my strings have been clipped, and I have been transformed and now constantly moving toward my destiny.

How will it impact the lives of others?

Once I got real about my lack of passion about computers and got real about my passion for people, that's when things started taking off for me. It's an eye-opener when you realize that you have been putting a lot of energy on the wrong path. Someone once asked, when did I realize what I should be doing? For me, it has not been some sort of overnight shift. This has been a calling that has been placed on my life for years, but it took a series of events to move me to a level of maturity to take action.

So to be clear, reader! You are my passion. If you are trying to figure out life or your next move, I am here to help. This will serve as a guide, but most of all, I want to connect my reality with yours. I will share my heart and enable you to connect with me, and I will share my journey. I want to instill in you that there is so much hope and possibility. All it takes is a shift in beliefs. Keep reading and get ready for your fantastic journey.

What are the claims of this thought training?

First of all, I promise NOT to motivate you. I think that term has been overused and quite frankly if you are looking to get motivated, why not just turn on some peppy pumped up music from Pandora. That will give you the same effect. No, I am more into, instead of motivation; I am into helping people discover their motives. Once you figure out why you are doing something, which will reveal what you would be doing and how you will get it done. Also, through a series of questions, I will challenge you to look deeper inside yourself and to take ownership of your destiny. I want to encourage you to take claim on your company. I want you to become the CEO of your life and your life-brand. This will be real and at times raw. It may open some wounds, but with the intent to heal things once and for all. So, from this point forward, I am asking you to be brave. It takes a brave person to look deep inside themselves and to be honest, real, raw and demand accountability, integrity, with the intent to change. Are you still with me?

How to use this guide:

This is a 6 week deep dive. Each week, you will get a different theme based on a core question. Each day of the week, you will have a focused time where you will be encouraged to explore and test a new topic. Much of this is excerpts from my personal journals where I have hard-core heart-to-heart coaching talks with myself. I have edited it and toned it down to make it palatable for a general audience. Also, at the top of the week, there will be a theme of thought. This will help you get your focus for what to expect for the week. Do that along with your top of the weekly assignment. Take your time to work through and journal your thoughts. You will do this for each week. Also, I would like for you to go to **AmericanGoGetter.com/BrandedandBold** and leave a comment and check out some of the supplemental videos. Also, make sure to register your email so you can be kept apprised of any new developments or webinars. You are going to love this interactive experience, and I am grateful to be your guide.

How to get out of your own way?

When you break down any change that you must go through, you must understand that your skills are limited to the present and the past. You have not experienced the future. So, your solutions are limited. For any moves you have made to develop a better and brighter future, your own hands have made the real hindrance. So, this training will grant you the tools and strategy of how to get out of your own way. You are your own worst enemy. So, we will, at times, go to battle with yourself. For, once you face the enemy within, you will find there is no other.

So get focused and real. You are about to roll in the mud. You will get dirty. You will get worn from the work, but I am committed to giving you the edge you so badly need in order to move your life ahead and to give you ownership of shaping your own destiny. Now turn the page and let's go to work!

WEEK 1 – THE DREAM

Bold Declaration #1 - **DREAM:** I will accept my divine DREAM without limits and seek every way possible to move them into reality.

My father passed away when I was 13, so most of my memories and time with him was of my younger years. One moment that really stands out was near the Christmas when I was 8.

The setting was the night of Christmas Eve of 1973. My mother and I had gone to Church to celebrate with other families, as we traditionally did. While we were gone, my dad went into Santa mode. He turned our entire basement into Santa's drop-off-point. So, as my mother and I arrived, we entered the house. There my dad was to greet us. He then said in a nonchalant tone, "You just missed him." "Who?" I said. My dad replied, "Santa! He came in and went downstairs then left." My eyes grew big, and my mom said, "Let's go see what he was up too, down there." So, I slowly went down because I was excited and didn't know what to expect. When I got three-fourths of the way down the stairs, my eyes caught a sight I would never forget. Literally, every toy I had ever wanted or mentioned to my parents was there. There was an official Lion's football uniform. I got a Rock-em Sock-em robot set. I got a bike, a Sit-N-Spin, a train set, an official Speed Racer electric slot car race set, and so much more. But the gift that would top them all was an electric guitar. It was a yellow and black 6-string. I was over-the-moon excited. I played with that toy the most. I think I drove my parents crazy, because I did not know any music, and I did not get any lessons, but I strummed on that thing as if I was a pro. I would imagine myself on stage in front of thousands, rocking it out. I had big dreams for myself and for places my music would take me. That dream was large, and it swelled like a balloon and was ready to ascend into the stratosphere.

The subtle winds came that was the beginning of the doubt storm. I had a series of people, throughout a period of time, who would come to me and indicate that I was not that great. They told me I lacked talent. They spoke fear deep into me and talked about how they or I would be nervous to be in front of a crowd. I had people speak to me about other things I needed to consider for work and career as I grew up. It felt as if the dreams of being an entertainer loaded itself up in that large hot air balloon and simply drifted away and all I could do is wave goodbye to it.

Why did I stop? Why did I give up on my dreams? Was it hard work, fear, pain frustration? No matter what it was, I allowed someone else's vision to overplay my vision of the possibilities. I stopped looking at what could be and started listened to what others wanted. But why? It was my dream. Why did I give it away?

What's a dream?

To many people dreams take on various meanings. Some view it at a glimpse into the future. Some view them as a form of communication of one's soul to another. Some view dreams as nothing more than electrical energy stirring in your body and activating memory and imagination and putting them in a story form that sometimes makes sense. No matter what, we can all agree that it is a gift given to mankind. We have the power as well as the gift to dream while sleeping and to dream while we are awake. We interchange the terms dreams and vision with ease of expression. When it comes to vision, that is something we are more empowered to command. We hear the word tossed around in relation to sight as well in companies that are trying to set a direction for what it will do and how it will serve as well as measurable goals it will reach. Dreams are a gift. In no uncertain terms, they granted an opportunity for awareness in our role we get to play in life. The dream moves beyond our natural understanding and limitations, and they move us to an area of our life where we get to play and create. Make something out of nothing.

Why are dreams important to our existence?

As a child, I loved to play outside. I loved to go traipsing in the woods and the swamp near my childhood home. Sometimes after a strong rain, the banks along the swamp would get muddy. On a dry day, you could walk with ease, but if you were to walk out there after a fresh rain, you could get stuck in the mud. It would take a lot of work and effort to get out. The risk was, you could end up muddy before it was all said and done. You needed force and momentum.

That's what a dream is to our existence. The universe knows when we're not up to par with what we should be doing. So, it sends dreams to haunt and taunt us to move out of the mud. It's an awful temptation to be granted a dream with deep clarity and then to never move toward it or have some sort of barrier between it and you. Going after dreams move us to an area of excitement. This is where we grow. You see, we don't grow by getting good at fulfilling others dreams. We help out and sustain the world, but each of us is endowed with dreams that we choose to either nurture or bring to life, or we let it die in the womb of our minds. Dreams represent a higher level of life. It is an extension of us. Our dreams are our figurative children we bring into this world and enable with a rich and powerful legacy. Expanding what and how we are along with fulfilling our calling.

Where did we learn to dream?

They said that a person's name feeds into the character that they will have. Give a child a less than a supportive name; they will struggle with the level of confidence they will have in themselves. Give a child a name of power and prominence from their culture, and they will fight to live up to it. Our names feed into our identity. We were given this early on and were taught to recognize it. Early on, we were given dreams to help us understand and interpret life. Dreams can be scary, and they can equally be exciting. Dreams come to us all the time. They are there to help and guide, protect and to prod. There is nothing like the feeling of a recurring dream that is full of the grandeur of what the future may hold. There is nothing scarier as a dream that comes at you with pending doom. A dream come from sparks of interpretation of what can and should be as well as what could be if we chose to do nothing. Dreams are choice reviews at a higher level. Dreams are science theory's that beg to be explored. Dreams demand research as well as answers. Dreams call and desire a response. Are you leading your dreams?

Are there signs that we've stopped dreaming?

"There is no way on earth this dream could ever come about." "I don't see how any of this could ever happen." "Frankly, I am scared to work on this and make this happen." "What if I fail?" That is, for the most part. A seed has been planted in you. As they nurture, seeds of fear and doubt are planted alongside your dreams. As dreams sprout, they start to produce hope. Yet, fear and doubt grow at the same rate. They disguise themselves as dreams and start to steal the nutrients and to choke off the hope of the dream slowly. If that dream is to survive, weeding must take place early one. If not, a dream will only go as far as hope is fed. Fear and doubt are designed to keep us in the practice of failure. It's just one more thing we can add to the list of what we could not do. We fall into line and stay in practice of limitations. ***But what if the universe, along with the dreams that we're grated, also gave us an ironclad guarantee that we could not fail? Then what would we do with that dream?***

How can we learn to dream again?

Success leaves clues and so do dreams. Each person on the earth was granted a root purpose which is to serve their fellow man. If you can recognize that, then you can move into a position to freely dream. What if, you viewed dreams as being like food? Your mind and body are the storehouse and distribution center of the food. The world around you is hungry and starving. They are in need of what you have to offer. What you have to offer could revolutionize the feeding process. You could produce food that not only feeds but also transform life into a better health. Yet, your dreams sit in a closed warehouse. No one has lined up or has even asked for what you have to offer because you have not opened up or stated that you have a dream. But what if you walked through your warehouse, examined your offering. Took a survey of the needs in your area. Invited a few in to sample your offering and tested their health results. Did it help? Were people blessed and moved by your actions? OK! Take more steps. Play with that dream. Invite more in. Get signs made and tell more about your offering. Make it your intent to empty your storehouse. Don't worry about running out. There is more food to come, but the supply will not get replenished until you start distributing. Take the risk!

Can we create our dreams?

The placebo effect is where drug developers do a double-blind test of a drug with claims that it will treat a particular disease. They take a group of patients and give some the real treatment and others, the give a simulated cure. Not knowing the outcome, they administered and measured the results over time. What the placebo effect proved in many cases, is that if you can sell enough hope to a patient, our bodies are fearfully and wonderfully made to the degree that we could synthesize (or create) what we need to produce our own cure without the aid of a drug, but simply armed with hope. What I am suggesting is you play with your hope. You are the author of your own story, and you get to choose your own destiny. Once you can believe that you have been living with someone else's limiting story, you can then choose to stop listening and even to change the story and then re-write yourself as the hero of your own adventure. Be bold and daring to get-up, go-out, and do something with your dreams. Your dreams give you the power to create. To bring something from nothing, in a sense, that it was never thought of until you chose to move it out of your head and into reality. Get loud and bold and speak your dreams into existence. The world is waiting for you

DREAM WEEK

For the next 7 days, you have work to do. I have to warn you that I am about to push you. It's time to get real about your dreams. Some of your dreams have not been seriously thought about, or they may have thought about it one time, but placed on a shelf to sit and collect dust. Some have been listening to lies and have shut your dreams down. Well, I am here to be your dream guide, but rest assure, we will not sleep and we will not sleepwalk. We will be wide-awake. We will get heightened and aware. We will take ownership of what we are thinking about. We will renew our commitment to our destiny and ourselves. We are not going to sit on the weigh side and let out dreams tease us and then drift away. We are going to take our dreams by the tail, pull and climb up on its back and grab its main and ride it. We are going to make our dreams work for us. Are you ready? Let's GO!

Curtis L. Walker

DAY 1 - PEACEFUL BLISS

Feels good. Doesn't it? To lay there and be swept away by the details of your dreams. It feels real. You feel like you are soaring in the sky like an eagle. As you zip through the clouds, it's as if you could float on them. It's a comfortable feeling. Unusual, but still comforting. Your dreams are you mental playground where you get to go and experience life without limits.

So, while you are there take some time and really look around. What do you notice? What do you see yourself doing? Who's in this dream with you? Have you had this dream more than once? Do you see yourself doing things that you have never done in reality? Are any of the experiences pleasurable or do you find them to painfully challenging? Are there any events that bring you overwhelming joy? If you let them, your dreams can teach you some things.

Your dreams are the place where you get to play with the possibilities of life. When you bring a level of consciousness into your dreams, you can then play a little. This is where you bring your imagination into your dream realm. In your imagination, you can consciously be doing anything in your dreams; this is where you let loose and take off the real limits. This becomes a dwelling point for your things. What you concentrate on generates power to transform into reality and trigger your efforts at a subconscious level.

The excitement happens when you start to realize that as you are sleeping, that you are really in dreams. As you progress through the dream process, speaks of reality creeps in. How are you doing this? I'm not supposed to be up here. What if I crash?

All of a sudden you wake up and you realize that it was all just a dream. But it felt so real. You then contemplate the possibilities of falling back to sleep and catching that same dream. It felt so good. What a gift. To live life without limits, where the only limitation existed within your own mind. You start to wonder if what your dreams could ever become a living possibility. What could you do to make it come true?

Conventional wisdom indicates that most things we dream are outside of our reach. Yet, there are those that have brought their dreams to fruition. What made it possible? Drive, determination, perseverance? No matter what it was, it put a strong taste in your mouth that there is a hint of a possibility that it COULD possibly happen. Rest with that. Allow your mind to drift down the path of hope. Take it for a spin. Let's see what happens.

> **Positive Affirmation:**
> **My dreams are a gift granted by the universe that allows me to connect to things that I am being encouraged and enabled to create.**

Self-Assessment Questions:

- How would you describe the difference between a hope, a wish and a dream?
- What is your lifelong dream?
- What goals have you wanted to achieve but never took action on?
- Do the goals that you dream about, frighten you?
- After dreaming do you make action plans for reaching your dreams?
- Have you dreamt of a goal or task that is moving that it shook you to your core?
- What would you tell your best friend about pursuing their dreams? Would you follow that same advice?
- What do you want to experience out of life?
- How do you want to grow?
- What do you want to be your life's contribution?

Branded and Bold Quotes:

- "The future belongs to those who believe in the beauty of their dream." – Eleanor Roosevelt
- "Follow your bliss and the universe will open doors where there were only walls." – Joseph Campbell
- "Twenty years from now you will be more disappointed by the things you didn't do than the ones you did. So throw off the bowlines. Sail away from safe harbor. Catch the trade winds in your sails. (Explore – Dream – Discover)" – Mark Twain
- "You are never too old to set another goal or to dream a new dream." – C.S. Lewis
- "Beauty begins the moment you decide to be yourself." – Coco Chanel
- "Doubt kills more dreams than failure ever will." – Unknown
- "By being yourself, you put something wonderful in the world that was not there before." – Edwin Elliot
- "Never give up on what you really want to do. The person with big dreams is more powerful than one with all the facts." – H. Jackson Brown Jr.
- If you don't build your dream, someone else will hire you to help them build theirs." - Unknown
- "Don't quit your daydream" - Unknown

Action Steps:
Recall your oldest and long standing dream or goal. Write it down. Think about the steps required to make it come true.

DAY 2 - ANOTHER REALITY

Have you ever allowed yourself to freely dream? I mean really dream. Like to the level where you felt like it was real. Have dreamt down to a level where you could taste it? Are you able to see it in vivid colors? What about the smells? There is nothing like dreaming of your mom making her famous sweet yeast rolls. Now that is a heavenly treat. That's the sweet spot. You are in a state of euphoria. Where you feel like the unbelievable could happen.

Then something happens to you that pulls you out of your dream state. You awakened to this same old reality. How cruel, the tricks that life can play on us. How could you be in a place that felt so great one moment and then rapidly shifts to this reality of life? The sad truth is, it's by design.

Our dreams are the playground of our mind. The place where we can go to create and become inspired. We solve problems and develop cures. In our dreams, we can make the world better. In our dreams, we are handed something crucial. The KEY! The key to taking what we have dreamed and move it into reality. But how?

How can we make something so beautiful which is also so far out of reach, be a part of this world? Simple! We do this by choice. We choose to interpret that dreams meaning and the value it was supposed to bring to this conscious world. In this state, we design and are inspired by faith to build.

Dreams are a gift handed down to us from the universe. Our dreams are designed to move, lift and inspire. The universe in itself is a work of art, and we are encouraged to emulate its features. We are teased and summoned to tap into our creativity. We are called to go on a quest and discover who we were meant to be. In our reality, we get to grind away the rough edges and bring forth our true identity. This is where we bring clarity to the true gift that the universe is daring to present to us. We are being challenged to either be adolescent in letting the dream remain a part of our imagination or step up to the next level and move it into reality.

So what will you do with this gift? Keep it warped or will you take it out and play with it? Will you take the plunge? Will you choose to lose all fears of what others may think and start to discover your truest dreams and bring it into the tangible present? You owe it to the world. You have a moral obligation to bless this place with the greatness of the experience of your dreams

---

Positive Affirmation:
You have a right, calling and moral obligation to bring your dreams into reality.

Self-Assessment Questions:

- If I put forth my best effort in my dreams, I should be able to produce in less than three months….?
- I need to sit down with…..and thank them for the work they have done up till now with my development.
- The following has been the on-going limitations to my stated dreams…..
- I have regularly performed the following actions that show I support my own dreams….
- I struggle with these stated realities in how they impact my ability to dream……
- The following activities have stretched me in how it made my dreams believable……
- The following things I hate to do also inspire and confirm that I am on the right path with pursuing my dreams…..
- Do you like to dream but not the hard work?
- How has it felt to see some of your dreams become a reality?
- Do you ever feel that there is something that is feeding your dream?

Branded and Bold Quotes:

- ➢ "Let us make our future now, and let us make our dreams tomorrow's reality." – Malala Yousaf Zai

- ➤ ➤ "A dream you dream alone is only a dream. A dream you dream together is a reality." – John Lennon
- ➤ ➤ "The distance between your dreams and reality is called discipline." – Unknown
- ➤ ➤ "It's the possibility of having a dream come true that makes life interesting." – Paulo Coelho
- ➤ ➤ "Each man should frame life so that at some future hour fact and his dreaming meet." – Victor Hugo
- ➤ ➤ "Reality is wrong. Dreams are for real." – Tupac Shakur
- ➤ ➤ "Don't downgrade your dream just to fit your reality. Upgrade your conviction to match your destiny." – Unknown
- ➤ ➤ A dream doesn't become reality through magic; it takes sweat, determination, and hard work." – Colin Powell
- ➤ ➤ What we achieve inwardly will change outer reality." – Plutarch

> **Action Steps:**
> **Write down and fully describe your life's dream a calling. List the require elements to make that dream come true.**

DAY 3 - SOUL FOOD

It hits your taste buds and moves you to a place. A place oh, so familiar. Home! The place where you were established and planted. They <u>move you</u> to a time when you felt like you could do anything. In that very moment, reflecting on sitting around the family table, you connect to the thoughts of what you hope to be.

A doctor, a lawyer, a firefighter, a superhero. You dreamed of places where you would go and things you would do. Those were dreams in their purest form. Untainted by fear, doubt, or failure. All there was, were the thoughts of what you wanted to do and your actions to make it happen. Fueled by you unclouded imagination.

What a gift? Why did we stop feeding? Did someone say that the mind food was bad for you? Was your dreaming causing you or someone else some sort of sickness? Check your pulse. Are you still breathing? Is your heart still beating? Then there is still hope.

The only thing that has changed between then and now is time. The dreams were a thought back then, and it's faint, but still a dream none the less. So, how can you rekindle your dream?

You take a visit back home to your metal heritage. Get small for a moment. Get childlike faith and embolden your beliefs. Wind the clock back for a moment and think back to that dream. Allow yourself to let it feel real. Think back to what made it real for you. Was it the atmosphere? Was it seeing others do what you thought you could do?

Think back to that dream. Let it feel like an ingrained memory. Like as if you were sitting at the table with your family gathered, and it's Thanksgiving. You finished the meal, and now it's time for that what you have been salivating. You have been smelling your favorite pie baking and cooling all morning long. You were so emotional about it that you could have skipped the dinner and went straight for the pie.

The Pie was brought out and set on the table before you. This anticipation was about to be over. You watched and the knife sliced through it as smooth as a hot knife cutting through butter. As it is being lifted it out, you feel moister forming in your mouth, anticipating the flavor. They slid a plate in front of you, and there is nothing in the way. This dream is about to get real. You dig in and take the first bite. Heaven! That's the feeling. This just connected with your soul. But this is not the pie, but it is your dream calling you.

From the past to right now. Did your memory die? Do you still desire? Did you let your childlike faith die as you got older? Why? It is only dead as long as you chose to let it be that way. Open up and take a bite. Make it real. Do something with it. Don't let your appetite be denied.

> **Positive Affirmation:**
> **Your dreams are as strong only as far as your desire to fulfill your appetite**

Self-Assessment Questions:

- For a long time, I have been wanting to fully engage in.......?
- When I think about the future, I would love to do.........?
- Are you giving yourself time and opportunity to dream about the future?
- If I don't live up to my dreams and potential, then I will deprive the world of......?
- Have your dreams caused you fear or anxiety that has held you back?
- What are the motives behind your dreams?
- How hungry are you about going after your dreams?
- I have to remove the following roadblock in order to see my dreams fulfilled. (1)...(2)…(3)…?
- Is your dream so real enough that you could taste it?
- Do you believe in your dreams enough to the point where you are ready to enlist the help of others so you can get there?
- My fulfilled dreams will benefit humanity by ……….?
- What have you learned about yourself as you have worked on your dream?
- How has working on your dream challenged you to grow?

- What do your dreams or desire say about you?
- Is there something in this world you have been longing to change?
- If you clearly know your goal and interest, what work have you done to help develop your dream into a reality?

Branded and Bold Quotes:

- "Be fearless in the pursuit of what sets your soul on fire." – Unknown
- "Maybe the journey isn't so much about becoming anything. Maybe it's about unbecoming everything that isn't really you, so you can be who you were meant to be in the first place." – Unknown
- "It is time to dream again. It is time to feed your soul." – Van Reagh
- "If one advances confidently in the direction of his dream, and endeavors to live the life which he has imagined, he will meet with a success unexpected in common hour." – Henry David Thoreau
- "It all starts with you. You're the temple, and you have control. Are you in a bad situation? It's up to you to get out of it. You can't give another human the responsibility for your happiness." – Taraji P. Henson
- Remember your dreams are as hungry as your demons. Make sure you're feeding the right ones." – Unknown
- "Faith doesn't make sense. It makes miracles." – Tony Evans
- 'This hope is a strong and trustworthy anchor for our souls." – Hebrews 6:19
- "Dip into your own soul. Find your own truth. What calls to your heart? What moves your

spirit? Make your life dance to the song of your own essence!" – Phillip Blanchett
- ➢ "My hunger for success is fueled by my passion" – Michelle Leilani
- ➢ "Dreams are illustrations from the book your soul is writing about you." – Marsh Norman

> **Action Steps:**
> **Write down your goals. Now prioritize. At the top of the list is the one that is the strongest. Focus on the one that you are most hungry about.**

DAY 4 - BEYOND BELIEFS

Many people have been stopped or shut down simply because they received the word from an EXPERT saying that they can't do anything. Well, what I am about to say next, may upset a few people, but the hard-cold truth is, there are no experts. There are only levels of beliefs. Now, give me about 60 seconds here for your mind to play with this thought. Don't totally dismiss it and checkout here. If you allow your higher conscious to kick in you will start to see that there is some truth to this.

You see, experts emerge from a series of trial and errors. The determination to reach a certain level and at the core, they got to their level based on a hypothesis that was fueled by a belief. However, that comes with a limitation. You see, a limitation is limited by time, space and the person that is at that given moment. That added to beliefs, determine if a person can break beyond a pre-determined belief. Take a look around you. All that have displayed before you have come from someone breaking past so-called experts and they went with their gut and acted according to what they believed.

So how does this apply to you? What limitation have you been choosing to consume? Do you find yourself standing in your same old tracks and not moving? Conforming to a role in society, because it is easy and convenient? You picked up this training because you are the type of person who senses a pull, or a higher calling if you will, which encourages you to act. It encourages you to do something. But what? The answer to this lies deep within. But many are afraid to explore the trust.

You see, we have been frightened to stay within the lies and comfort. Experts have told us that life should only be a certain way. However, who gave them that permission and authority over our lives? And, quite frankly, are they really rocking out their own lives, while trying to dogmatically tell you how to live your own? I challenge you today to not only know what you believe, but master what you believe, and challenge it to it's the highest degree. Test it and see if there are areas where it and you can grow. Remember, your own beliefs only limit you.

Positive Affirmation:
Remember, you are only limited by your own beliefs

Self-Assessment Questions:

- List things that you have been successful at?
- What things have you struggled with but yet managed to accomplish?
- I have been stopped so may time by the following in the past....?
- Describe your beliefs when it comes to the goals that you want to reach.
- What transformation do you expect by reaching your goals?
- Is reaching your goal also a need?
- How will you honestly know that you have done your personal best at reaching your goals?
- Describe what it would feel like to tie your personal beliefs to the goals you are trying to hit.
- What difference would it make if you reached your goal or not?
- What could persuade you to give up on your dreams?
- Do you see any of your life's purpose associated with this goal you are trying to reach?
- If you knew you could not fail what would you do next?
- Life is trial and error: What can you do differently to get new and better results?

Branded and Bold Quotes:

- You are braver than you believe, stronger than you seem and smarter than you think. – Brian Tracy
- "The only thing limiting us in life is our belief that there are limits." – Harlee Wallace
- "Worry does not empty tomorrow of its sorrow. It empties today of its strength." – Corrie Ten Boom
- "Don't let small minds convince you that your dreams are too big." - Unknown
- "It is not the stars to hold our destiny but in ourselves." – William Shakespeare
- "Dreams come in size too big so we can grow into them." – Josie Bisset
- "You can't put a limit on anything. The more you dream, the farther you get." – Michael Phelps
- "Don't give up on your dreams, or your dreams will give up on you." – John Wooden
- "The biggest adventure you can take is to live the life of your dreams." – Oprah Winfrey
- "Believe in your dreams. They were given to you for a reason." – Katrina Mayer

Action Steps:
Reflect on things you have been told NO about and examine your personal conviction. Question that NO and find a way to get it done. Don't think. DO!

DAY 5 - PROBLEMS SOLVED

Your beliefs only limit you. Seriously! Think about some of the amazing things that you see people do, such and operate on a baby, while it is still in the womb. Space-age medicines that were never heard of 30 years ago. Cars that can stop themselves in the event of an emergency. These things were never heard at certain points and time, and there were those that were strong in their position that said these things could and never should be done. Yet, it took someone with a small spark of belief. Someone who would play with the possibilities and began by formulating a strong hypothesis that led to a small step of action that then began to drive them to the point of reality.

Problems! What are these? Nothing more than temporary obstacles wrapped in a story. To quickly move the obstacles, simply change the story. Your conscience does not know any different. But once you start to believe the story, of success over obstacles, then you will be able to tap into your ultimate creativity and fine artistic means to eliminate your opposition and remove all challenges.

Problems are no more than a school-yard bully. Walking around loud and taking up space. Way more space than allotted. Picking the weak to prey upon. Rumors drive the power of that bully. Yes, this bully has power, but this bully also has limits. Once a person with courage chooses to stand up and face this bully, that's when the story starts to change. When this bully is faced, the long-standing chains break and fall off. When you stand up to a bully, you inspire others to stand up as well. So, refuse to take it any further. Don't give in. Jump into this fight.

So release your thoughts. Think high and think big. Think free. Unleash your mind on anything that is standing in your way. Visualize the problem being solved. See it being eradicated. Fight for your vision. Make it a reality. And on that glorious day in the future, you can look at what you conceived and say, "Problem Solved!"

Positive Affirmation:
The power of a problem is weaken by the power of resistant-apposing beliefs.

Self-Assessment Questions:

- What are my usual excuses for why I don't have what I desire?
- How many times have my limiting thoughts impacted my life?
- Is there a pattern of my limiting thinking?
- Do I really want to have this problem solved or do I enjoy talking about the problem?
- Who do I really want to be?
- If I honestly addressed my problems, how would I view myself?
- How do I want to show up when facing my problems?
- What role does fear play in your decision to address your problems?
- What is most threatening in this situation? What is "safe"?
- Who will I potentially be threatening by choosing to address obstacles and opposition in my life?
- What will you lose when you get what you want?
- What influences, control, privileges, relationships or money would you have to give up, in order to solve this problem or fulfill your desire?
- Whose permission do you need to address issues that are in front of you?
- How am I enabling that person to control me?
- What do I need from them? Who else can support me? Do I support them?

- Limitations! – If I had to live like this for the next year, 10 years, or till I'm 90 – am I OK with this?
- What would my life be like if no one could intimidate me again? (Not because I'm threatening, but because I have peace and power within me and I accept myself completely)
- List things that you have been successful at?
- What things have you struggled with but yet managed to accomplish?

Branded and Bold Quotes:

- "Don't be pushed by your problems. Be led by your dreams." – Ralph Waldo Emerson
- "I don't fix problems, I fix my thinking, then problems fix themselves" – Louise L. Hay
- "The secret of change is to focus all of your energy, not on fighting the old, but on building the new." – Socrates
- "Let us make our future now, and let us make our dreams tomorrow's reality." – Malala Yousafzai
- "Complaining about a problem without posing a solution is called whining." – Teddy Roosevelt.
- "We cannot solve our problems with the same mind we used when we created them." – Albert Einstein
- "With ordinary talent and extraordinary perseverance, all things are attainable." – Thomas Fowell Buxton

- "God gives talent. Work transforms talent into genius." – Anna Pavlova
- "One moment can change a day, one day can change a life, and one life can change the world." – Buddha
- "Scientist dream about doing great things. Engineer do them." – James A. Michener

> **Action Steps:**
> **Write down and describe what it would look like and feel like to have the problem before you, solved. Read it 4 times a day. See what your brain comes up with to help solve the problem.**

DAY 6 - WORTH PURSUING

When you think of being in pursuit of something it implies that there is a target. Something you are going after, a goal you want to achieve, or a next-level plateau you want to achieve. Also, it implies that there may be obstacles. The obstacles may be real or perceived. Obstacles are a limitation that MUST be worked past. Ultimately it will require a change in order to hit that mark.

Your ability to hit that mark rest on some key elements. Your focus is one. If you don't have a clearly defined focus, then you leave room for distractions to take over your journey and practices required to get you to the end goal. So you have to identify your target and map out the path it takes to get there. Along with that focus, you MUST have an insatiable hunger or appetite that will compel you to work past all odds and obstacles. It has to be strong enough to sustain you through the trials that stand before you.

Along with that MUST is a huge dose of excitement. Hitting your target has to move you to an emotional level. This goal has to resonate with your spirit and anchor in such a way that it helps define your very being. It has to move you to a state of self-reflection. Where you get to see yourself and your role in life that you must play to yourself as well as to others.

But know this. The journey and change will not be easy. It is asking more of you in a way that others won't do. It is moving you out of your comfort zone. It will place demands on your character. It will chisel and grind away at what is weak and could potentially hold you back. You may be required to let people, things and activity go for a season in order to hit y our mark.

It will challenge you to change your natural perception of life. It will narrow things down to a choice, habit, and courage. Your target is your choice. No one else's. You have to put in the work to make it. Then you have to examine your habits to see what works and what does not. Then you have to take action. The courage to take a leap of faith.

So, are you hungry? Are you ready to get into the fight for your life? Today is the first day of the rest of your life. Now get up and make it happen.

Positive Affirmation:
Your goals are not going to find themselves. You've got to set them. Get them in sight. Hunt them down and execute them. Claim your prize!!

Self-Assessment Questions:
- Do you really want it? Really?
- What are you willing to sacrifice?

- Which doors will close by accepting this pursuit?
- Do the little things excite you?
- How much will it hurt to pursue your goals?
- Is it worth those hardest moments?
- What does ultimate success feel like, what does it taste like?
- Are you afraid of succeeding?
- Do you have the support you need to get you through?
- Does it feel good to share your pursuit with others?
- Would you enjoy giving a loved one the honest explanation for why you gave up?
- Are you ready to stand up to the people who will try to knock you down?
- Why did you want to pursue this goal, to begin with, and has anything changed?
- Did you set a smart goal? SMART goals are: (Specific, Measurable, Attainable, Realistic, Time-bound)
- Would your life be better if you gave up on this goal?
- What would you tell someone else if they were in your shoes?

Branded and Bold Quotes:

- "Sometimes life is about risking everything for a dream no one can see but you."
- "If it's both terrifying and amazing then you should definitely pursue it." – Erada

- "Never give up on a dream just because of the time it will take to accomplish it. The time will pass away." – Unknown
- "All our dreams can come true if we dare to pursue them. " Walt Disney
- "Stay focused, go after your dreams and keep moving toward your goals." – LL Cool J
- "Don't watch the clock; do what it does. Keep going." – Sam Levenson
- "Believe in yourself! Have faith in your abilities! Without a humble but reasonable confidence in your own powers, you cannot be successful or happy." – Norman Vincent Peale
- "The time will pass away. You can either spend it creating the life you want or spend it living the life you don't want. The choice is yours."
- "The positive thinker sees the invisible, feels the intangible, and achieves the impossible." – Winston Churchill
- "Don't wait; the time will never be 'just right.' Start where you stand, and work with whatever tools you may have at your command, and better tools will be found as you go along." – George Herbert

---

Action Steps:
Don't just think about your goal. Take action. Within the next hour do at least 1 thing that will move you closer to your goal.

DAY 7 – REJOICE IN IT

Dreaming is a gift. If you have a dream, it means that the universe has not forsaken you. To dream, for some, can be frustrating. For many have been persuaded not to take action on the dreams they have been granted. This has to lead to heartbreak to see something so vividly but never taking the leap to make it a functional reality of your existence. But I can say, there is nothing like the feeling of throwing caution into the wind, and stopping and giving thanks for what you have experienced in life and learning to celebrate the moments and finding solace and energy in that moment of praise to give you the fuel you need to take that next step of faith.

Allow me, if you will, to dwell on a word of significant power. That word is GRATITUDE!. So what does it mean to live with gratitude? Being in a state of mind where you look at EVERYTHING as a gift. Good and bad, you take in and process. You fight the natural urge to count your failures, but you elevate your thinking and look at every event to be a gift of development. Miracles if you will.

It takes a mature mind to interpret setbacks as gifts of progress. Events are nothing more than data that feed our beliefs. We get to interpret that information to shape our beliefs over time. It takes a trained eye to see progress and setbacks and miracles. These events shape our overall story. It's one thing to succeed right out the gate, with your errors or hiccups, but it's quite another thing to experience setbacks, and through them, you acquire a new level of strength, and you anchor deeper to the very thing you've dreamed about. The thing that separates failure from success is simply the interpretation of our life events.

To rejoice and live with gratitude requires you to shift your focus. It changes what you dwell on and how you dwell on it. It changes how you manage your time and energy. If you are in a state of gratitude, you can then quickly let go of what's not working and move to what is gaining you ground and enabling you to experience joy and satisfaction.

Having gratitude enables you to quickly reframe any potential negative situation into something from which you gain power and knowledge. Enemies don't harm you; they encourage you to get better. Obstacles don't cripple you; they help you find your strength to move forward.

Imaging all that you have, right now, immediately taken from you. Heath, wealth, people, position and reputation. The feeling could be devastating. Now, imagine how you would feel if it all gradually came back to you. How overwhelmed would you be? With that same level of emotion, how much more excited are you about the gains of tomorrow in how you will go after and pursue your dreams. Take advantage of your attitude of gratitude. Dreaming is a gift. If you have a dream, it means that the universe has not forsaken you. To dream, for some, can be frustrating. For many have been persuaded not to take action on the dreams they have been granted. This has to lead to heartbreak to see something so vividly but never taking the leap to make it a functional reality of your existence. But I can say, there is nothing like the feeling of throwing caution into the wind, and stopping and giving thanks for what you have experienced in life and learning to celebrate the moments and finding solace and energy in that moment of praise to give you the fuel you need to take that next step of faith.

Allow me, if you will, to dwell on a word of significant power. That word is GRATITUDE!. So what does it mean to live with gratitude? Being in a state of mind where you look at EVERYTHING as a gift. Good and bad, you take in and process. You fight the natural urge to count your failures, but you elevate your thinking and look at every event to be a gift of development. Miracles if you will.

It takes a m   t setbacks as gifts of progress. Events are nothing more than data that feed our beliefs. We get to interpret that information to shape our beliefs over time. It takes a trained eye to see progress and setbacks and miracles. These events shape our overall story. It's one thing to succeed right out the gate, with your errors or hiccups, but it's quite another thing to experience setbacks, and through them, you acquire a new level of strength, and you anchor deeper to the very thing you've dreamed about. The thing that separates failure from success is simply the interpretation of our life events.

To rejoice and live with gratitude requires you to shift your focus. It changes what you dwell on and how you dwell on it. It changes how you manage your time and energy. If you are in a state of gratitude, you can then quickly let go of what's not working and move to what is gaining you ground and enabling you to experience joy and satisfaction.

Having gratitude enables you to quickly reframe any potential negative situation into something from which you gain power and knowledge. Enemies don't harm you; they encourage you to get better. Obstacles don't cripple you; they help you find your strength to move forward.

Imaging all that you have, right now, immediately taken from you. Heath, wealth, people, position and reputation. The feeling could be devastating. Now, imagine how you would feel if it all gradually came back to you. How overwhelmed would you be? With that same level of emotion, how much more excited are you about the gains of tomorrow in how you will go after and pursue your dreams. Take advantage of your attitude of gratitude.

Positive Affirmation:
If it does not make you excited about enough to get you out of the bed and go for it, then it may not be for you.

Self-Assessment Questions:
- What opportunities do you feel like you have missed out on?

- Do you think there is time to give it another go?
- Have you set too high of ambition for your goal? Have you made any attempts at it?
- Are you able to see any level of progress or growth from the attempts or failures?
- Describe how you hope to feel when you reach your ultimate goals?
- While reviewing your dreams did you discover what your true passion may be?
- While in pursuing your dreams, what areas have you been challenged to display courage?
- As you pursue your goals have you taken note of the type of person you are and consider the person you will be?
- Is there any level of gratitude in your heart?
- Have you taken inventory of your past success and has that provided inspiration to what you will do in the future?
- You only really have today. You don't have tomorrow. So in this moment, what victories can you give an account to, that you can clearly say that you are happy about?
- Do you struggle with being happy in the moment? Why?
- In what ways are you letting your attitude shape your day instead of letting your day and events shape you?
- Are you excited about what is getting ready to happen in your life?

Branded and Bold Quotes:

- "Make a conscious effort to surround yourself with positive, nourishing, and uplifting people. People who believe in you, encourage you to go after your dreams, and applaud your victories." – Jack Canfield
- "You can complain that roses have thorns, or rejoice that thorns have roses." _ Zig Ziglar
- "Your life is your message to the world. Make sure it's inspiring."
- F-E-A-R has two meanings: 'Forget Everything And Run' or 'Face Everything And Rise." – The choice is yours."
- "The more you praise and celebrate your life; more there is in life celebrate." – Oprah Winfrey
- "Don't tell people your dream. Show them!"
- Happiness is letting go if what you think life is supposed to look like and celebrating it for everything that it is."
- "Somewhere inside all of us is the power to change the world." – Roald Dahl
- 'Every flower of every tomorrow are in the seeds of today."
- "Your life has a purpose. Your story is important. Your dreams count. Your voice matters. You were born to make an impact."

Action Steps:
Stand to your feet and move around and say with energy, what your goals and intentions are. Say it so it can heard in the next galaxy.

WEEK 2 – THE AWAKENING

Bold Declaration #2 - **AWAKE:** I will **AWAKEN** to my true calling and pursue it with relentless passion

You made it through week one. Where you honest with yourself? Did you do the work? Did you step up and take actions. Dreaming is critical to allowing yourself permission to succeed. Dreaming is a gift. The spiritual playground of the universe where you are enticed to be more than you think you could ever become. Do, did you play. If you struggled with any of the assignments, take some time to review. Go back and do it again. Get comfortable and familiar with it. You see, it is foundational for the next step I am about to lead you into.

Now that you have been dreaming, it is time to wake up. Here is where things get exciting. This is where you test yourself to see if you can move to the next level of life.

This is where you do some next level imagination. Thinking higher about your possibility and destiny. This is where you examine if you are mastering your destiny or if you are being a puppet that is following the path of the strings.

Bear in mind; there is nothing wrong with someone helping construct a career path for you. Your parents or guidance counselor may have provided you suggestions and may have even opened some doors for you, but ultimately, you have to do the work. So, if you had to do what was suggested for the next 20 years, would you be happy and satisfied? If not, then let's wake up and do some research. Let's seek out and find our true calling.

There is some unwritten agreement that many have been operating under that was not governed, or the terms agreed to. It's as if many were functioning under a hypnotic trance. A life managed is not a full life. Especially when we discover that we are not the ones managing our own life. To a degree, it is right and respectable to have a certain aspect of your life managed, such as if you are in the military. There has to be certain level of conformity in order to establish a baseline for teamwork and team commitment, but the one thing I discovered when I served my country, was that they also encouraged me to learn and master my own personal gifts and identity so that I could show up every day and bring my best tools into service.

When we are wide awake, we are in a state where you clearly know who we are and have pushed the parameters of our calling. We get to recognize where we fit and where we don't fit. We identify things that need to change in order for us to adjust to where our destiny is taking us. We can be a part of a team and at the same time be totally different, fulfilling a global and individual purpose.

In order to move from a state of sleep to fully awake, it may require a nudge. Some may call it a CALLING. That voice that says the dream was cool, but it is not where you belong. It is calling us to feel that if that dream was so great, why leave it in the dream world? Why not step up and work life in such a way that you bring features of that dream into reality. Your own thoughts only limit you.

There are times when we wake from a dream and wonder where we are because the level of dreams was so intense that it altered your sense of reality. You lost sight of where you were. Like a dream, when you come to the point of self-actualization, we open our eyes and say, what have I been doing with my life? This is not what I envisioned. It's time to make some changes. So, what shall you do? The real questions and answers lay inside. So, let's explore.

Don't hit the snooze. Time to get up and take action

DAY 8 - CRUSH THE CONTRACT

When did it become OK to be average? I bet if I were to ask this question to most people, the first response would be that they are not average. Many are going to or have gone to school to get a diploma, degree or certificate. Some have gone after the job that looked promising. Most people take that route, and there is nothing wrong with that route. But there is an area of concern if you did it without deep self-examination.

There is something morally wrong if you have a calling or a pulling on your life that indicates you should be working on something specific, yet you chose to stick within the safety of the status quota. It's as if someone has hypnotized you and took over your mind and sent your body on a path, not of your own choosing, yet you are slightly conscious and aware, while inside, kicking and screaming. Wanting to get out and break free. Yet the boundaries of fear have kept you restricted to the chosen path.

But who chooses the path and why? Does this path agree with your soul? Does it resemble your calling or can it be used a stepping stone to your calling? If not, then why are you accepting it? Did someone write a contract with you and presented the terms and you discovered that you didn't agree to the terms because they insulted the giant that was growing within?

Are you functioning as if they had the audacity to take your hand and put a pen in it and forced you to sign that document, condemning you to a life of hallowed existence? If this is resonating with you, then take a moment to examine this next statement. TEAR IT UP! You don't have to live under those terms. (Disclaimer: This is a figurative contract. If you are in the military, then it may not be a good idea to tear up your contract and walk away from your responsibility. That may not go over to well. Just saying). Unless you are a prisoner in a cell chained to a wall 24by7, you have no real excuse to make a decision and to take action to alter and take mastery of your own life and destiny.

Now, I am not promoting getting angry at your parents or others who have encouraged or supported you along the way, up until this moment. But I am asking you to, out of respect, take a moment to make a new plan and define a better contract that feeds who you are and who you want to become. Be mature and take responsibility. Responsibility is not some hollow word, but it symbolizes real and meaningful action. Your contract and commitment to yourself should be an unrelenting action that you take on your dreams and goals until the day you arrive. Make no excuses and don't settle. Don't do it for anyone else, unless that person is your future self. Do

---

Positive Affirmation:
Start a coup. Take over the helm of your life. Steer a course to greatness. Proceed with reckless abandon. Live!

something today, that your future self will thank you for.

Self-Assessment Questions:

- Who has been responsible for the changes and development up to now, in your life?
- If things go bad in y our life, who do you usually blame?
- For the success in your life, who has put in the bulk of the work? Who should have put in the bulk of the work?
- Do you find yourself going along with the flow of life or do you have a vision that you operate out of?
- Do you have people in your life that distract you from working on reaching your goals?
- What steps are you willing to take to cut off everything in your life that is not working?
- Do you begin your day with a purpose or are your plan and purpose dictated by someone else?
- How comfortable have you allowed yourself to become with your current role in life?
- What are your thoughts when it comes to discomfort associated with making progress in your life?
- What are you willing to go through to get to what you want?
- How committed are you to the thing that you are passionate about?
- What has convinced you to give up in the past?

- Do you take more mental inventory of your past, present or your future?
- What is a lasting impression you would like to leave in this world?

Branded and Bold Quotes:

- "If you're searching for that one person that will change your life, take a look in the mirror."
- "Few are those who see with their own eyes and feel with their own hearts." – Albert Einstein
- "The first step in crafting the life you want is to get rid of everything you don't want"
- "One small positive thought in the morning can change your whole day."
- "You will never find something better if you stay in your comfort zone."
- "Be loyal to your future, not your past."
- "Balance is not something you find. It's something you create."
- "When you arise in the morning, think of what a precious privilege it is to be alive – to breathe, to think, to enjoy, to love." – Marcus Aurelius
- "Don't start your day with broken pieces of yesterday. Every day is a fresh start. Each day is a new beginning. Every morning we wake up is the first day of our new life."
- "Be more concerned with our character than with your reputation." – John Wooden

Action Steps:
Kill your distractions. People, events, or things that don't fit with developing your goals or a better you, serve notice and cut ties. Free yourself to move forward.

DAY 9 - DARE TO BE DIFFERENT

What's wrong with being average? Nothing, if you are OK with settling and choosing to receive based on the limitations of others. Yet, inside there is a spirit that lies inside of each of us that calls out for more. You see, we all have a tendency to seek the average because it gives us just enough edge to get by. It puts us at a level of life where we don't have to deal with too much discomfort.

If we stick with what the crowd is doing we get to be nice, quiet, spectators of life that other people are playing and living with the longing to be on the field, but at the same time telling the story of limitations as to why we have not done what it takes to play in the game of life. However, our soul calls out and indicates to us that we should be more than average. This is where you should be zigging where you could have been zagging.

It takes a shift in mindset to be above average. Before the mind can shift, it has to start with a question? Are you satisfied with the current condition of your life? Do you feel that there is something more you should be engaging in? Who will you offend, if you choose to do something completely different? As you dig into the content that these questions produce you will find that the life you are living, and the way that most people live, is conditioned to fit in and be average.

However, those that are getting exceptional results for their lives, have asked these questions and then, they took the next step. They got up and started pursuing the life that was meant for them. They set aside excuses. They focused on what they wanted. They silenced the nay-sayers and readjusted their circle of influences. They went to work on themselves. They got real with themselves, their situation and were clear, honest and exact about what they wanted.

They then made a commitment to get in the habit of taking action and pressing forward, thru, pain, frustration, setbacks, criticisms, failures, and shame, in order to carve out the life that had been plaguing their dreams.

You see, once you get a taste of a dream, and it haunts you on a regular, you can't ignore something like that. The average person will say, that's too hard or out of my reach, but to the true visionary, they know to respond to that call. They know they have to be different than the mold that was set before them. Instead of letting events shape themselves, they choose to alter their beliefs about events and shape their own destiny. So, will you dare to be different?

Positive Affirmation:
Be intentional about being different or weird. Know and be what you have to become in order to fulfill your calling.

Self-Assessment Questions:

- I am unique in the following areas……?
- I have the natural ability to perform…….?
- In what areas of your life do you feel alive when you apply your gifts?
- Do you ever feel like you are emulating someone else's life instead of carving out your own?
- Do you view yourself as a pioneer?
- How well do you know yourself?
- What steps have to take to discover your true calling?
- What one thing you can do today that will benefit you in the future?
- What is your biggest struggle with understanding yourself and designing your future?
- Review all the past struggles. What have you learned about yourself through them?
- What examples are you leaving for others?
- Through your actionable steps, what have you inspired others to do?
- Are there any distractions that are keeping you from focusing on your development?
- What can you do to address the distractions?

Branded and Bold Quotes:

- "By doing what you love, you inspire & awaken the hearts of others."
- "You will never influence the world by being just like it."
- "Why fit in when you were born to stand out!" – Dr. Seuss

- "The biggest challenge of life is to be yourself in a world that is trying to make you like everyone else."
- "Do something today that your future self will thank you for."
- "Difficult roads often lead to beautiful destinations."
- "The rockiest roads lead to the highest peaks."
- "The best view comes after the hardest climbs."
- "I am a lighthouse rather than a lifeboat. I do not rescue, but instead help others to find their own way to shore, guiding them by my example."
- "Don't look back you're not going that way."

Action Steps:
Define the changes you may need to make in order to become the person you were called to be. Take immediate action on any one of the changes you must make.

DAY 10 - NO APOLOGIES

To apologize for something is to openly express your regret for any actions or lack of action you took to a given outcome that may have cause discomfort. Some have also associated the word apology for the word excesses. I get it when, by accident, you cause harm, which you must acknowledge your part that you played, but let's stop for a moment. What was the hurt that you caused? Was it a disappointment because your choices did not measure up to their expectation? Were your choices designed for improvement of self or was it frivolous and without regards for its lasting impact?

Before you can start handing out apologies, you have to consider all parties involved. First, you will have your offended party. They may have had wishes and dreams of what you were to do or accomplish and your actions did not measure up. But don't neglect the number one person that you have to face on a daily basis when it comes to disappointment. Yourself. You see, it takes an advanced and highly mature person to see that they must take ownership and get into a higher level of agreement with themselves. Then and only then should you place yourself in position to align yourself with someone else. To thine own self, be true.

I am encouraging you to heighten your awareness of the decisions you are making. In addition, I am encouraging you to look at the big picture as you move from managed to focus driven. This transition should not be done as an assault toward those that genuinely care about your future and development. If you have those kinds of people, you need to thank them. There has to be a level of respect granted as you make your decision because those that have been in your corner are at lease due some assurance that you are being responsible and well thought out in your decision.

What I am encouraging is, for you to take a higher level of responsibility. We proposed this earlier, but to go deeper, I had indicated that responsibility and action go hand and hand. The contrast is irresponsibility and the stories that go along with it. You, see, the high achievers in this world, they have learned to incorporate a habitual lifestyle that is stoked with a high amount of action. They think, but they don't do too much of that because they engage unapologetically.

The action is the core of their day. The take their cues from their vision and pull it out of the stratosphere and draw it down to earth and build, and chiseled on it daily, till one day, the dream becomes a reality. They don't apologize or make excuses. They don't sit around telling stories about their failure until after they have produced success.

A story without producible works is meaningless. Therefore, commit today to STOP the stories of what you can't do, or who is holding you back. Get up and take action! Your destiny has been calling. Why haven't you answered? Pick up the receiver and answer "YES!"

Make an agreement with yourself that you will no longer make an excuse and that you will move heaven and earth to make your dreams a reality. Agree with your soul. You only have today. You don't get tomorrow. So, put all the action that you can into today. Let the sound of you taking action drown out that of you wanting to whimper or make excuses. And trust me, excesses sounds like complaints and to be frank; no one wants to hear it.

> **Positive Affirmation:**
> **Be completely honest with yourself and then you will be able to see what you need to do and why it must be done. Let that define your convictions.**

Self-Assessment Questions:

- Do you ever find yourself apologizing for decisions you are making related to your life-plan development?
- What steps are you taking to prove you are responsible for your decisions?
- How resourceful have you been with addressing tough matters in the past?
- How do you view the power of fear?
- Is fear, in itself a right or wrong (good or bad) thing to you?
- What method do you use to overcome fear and place it in its rightful place?

- In what ways do you find yourself trying to fit in or going with the flow?
- Are there notable things holding you back from reaching your desires?
- What things or habits could you give up that could move you a little bit closer to your mark?
- When your experience the anxiety of change, do you find yourself also procrastinating?
- What are some steps you MUST absolutely take in order to experience success?
- Are you allowed to make alterations to your life-plan?
- Whose permission do you need to have in order to make changes for YOUR future?
- What governs your decisions the most: Hope or Fear?

Branded and Bold Quotes:

- "The best apology is a changed behavior"
- "If it is important to you, you will find a way. If not, you will find an excuse."
- "Hope is the only thing stronger than fear."
- "Don't waste a moment of your life trying to be normal"
- "If you want to fly, give up everything that weighs you down."
- "Make no apologies for setting high standards.

> "Remember that nothing would get done at all if a person waiting until he could do it so well that no one could find fault with it." – Sheila Waters
> "If you want to make a real change you have to go from saying 'I should' to saying 'I must." – Tony Robbins
> "This is my life…my story…my book. I will no longer let anyone else write it; nor will I apologize for the edits I make." – Steve Maraboli
> "May your choices reflect your hopes, not your fears." – Nelson Mandela

**Action Steps:
Stand in the mirror and make a personal commitment to yourself that you will endure the pain and press forward. Promise yourself that you won't back down. You own it to your future self.**

DAY 11 - WHAT'S CALLING YOU?

One of the surest ways to miss your calling is to never take time to do a mental check-in. Talking a good examination of how you feel in regards to your personal happiness. Happiness is an emotional indicator that lets you know when you are experiencing a moment of fulfillment. It's taking a look at the current life plan you are living and verifying if that plan matches up to the one you wanted.

You see if a person thoughts, words, and actions are out of sync then you will also find a person who is not on the path of their calling. A calling is something that touches us all at a spiritual level. To have engaged with the thoughts of your calling means that you have moved from a passive passenger in your own life, and now have moved over to the driver's seat. You are there, but you still may need to acquire the skills to drive as well as a destination to move your life-vehicle.

We, humans, have plateaus of living and expressing. Based on how we face challenges in life determine how we assess or defend those levels. It's in our DNA to grow. From birth, we had a passion to walk, run, eat, dress and over time we find new levels to climb. Why? Because we can. We were not designed to just go with the flow. That is why after we eat, there is a period of time where we feel satisfied, but that only last for a moment. We eventually crave more.

To explore your calling, take a few minutes to examine what really matters to you. Ask yourself, if you had 7 years remaining in your life, what would you try to pack into this period of time? Who would you talk to? What would you accomplish? What if, instead of 7 years, you were only given 7 months? How would your answers change? What if it was 7 weeks? 7 days? 7 minutes? When you break it down, it helps you discover your importance as well as what is the focus of your true calling. If you discovered that you had a certain thing on your list, that no matter the amount of time you had, that item never changed, then that is a clue to what your calling may be.

Discovering your calling is important, but not as much as how you will answer. Your action is your answer. So, what action will you take today?

> **Positive Affirmation:**
> **If you have been thinking about something for a long time and it haunts you, then that's the calling you really need to root out and define, and but your honest effort in pursuit.**

Self-Assessment Questions:

- What are the challenges or obstacles that stand before you on the path to your goal?
- Have you identified methods to remove your obstacles?
- Who are the mentors or examples that have gone before you that have effectively addressed similar challenges?
- How do you examine your level of excitement related to why you are pursuing your goal?
- How would you finish this sentence: I have discovered my true calling to be……?
- On a scale from 1 to 10, where 1 is low, and 10 is high, how excited are you about the outcome of pursuing your passion?
- In your daily review of your goals, what steps are you taking to promote clarity about where you're at with your goal pursuit and how much more ground do you need to cover to get there?
- Can you clearly define what it is you want or what you want to become?
- In the pursuit of your goal, in what areas of your life have you noticed maturity and growth?
- Do you feel it is necessary to know in detail all that you must do well before you take any action? How is that working for you?
- What sacrifices have you made in order to pursue your goal up to this point? What sacrifices do you need to make?

- When you take action toward your goals, in what areas of your life do you feel inspired?
- How do you manage your urge to procrastinate?
- What are the positive emotions you feel when actively working on your goals?
- Are there people in your life that have gone all-out in the pursuit of their goals? How has that inspired you to take action?
- What can be done to solidify your commitment to your own success?
- In what way is your journey like an adventure?

Branded and Bold Quotes:

- "Challenges are here to awaken you, and even if you're awakening, life continuously gives you challenges, and then the awakening accelerates and deepens.' – Eckhart Tolle
- "Follow your bliss and the universe will open doors where there were only walls." – Joseph Campbell
- "When you're clear about what you want it's amazing how quickly life can rearrange itself to make your dream a reality." – Melani Beckler
- "What lies behind you and what lies in front of you, pales in comparison to what lies inside of you." – Ralph Waldo Emerson
- "Faith is taking the first step even when you don't see the whole staircase." – Martin Luther King Jr
- "You have to go wholeheartedly into anything in order to achieve anything worth having." – Frank Lloyd Wright

- "The greatest privilege of human life is to become a midwife to the birth of the soul."
- "Sometimes the smallest step in the right direction ends up being the biggest step of your life."
- "I don't know what my calling is, but I want to be here for a bigger reason. I strive to be like the greatest people who have ever lived." – Will Smith
- "Adventure may hurt you, but monotony will kill you."

Action Steps:
Review your dreams and journal and look for reoccurring patterns. This is where you will find your hidden treasure. Now dig it up!

DAY 12 - TURN THE PAGE

Goals and Focus – What gets your attention, gets you. If you are focusing on why you failed or why you are stuck in life, the more you will develop reasons not to move forward. Your mind is your most valuable assets. It functions by its give queue. It has the power to create as well as the power to destroy. Your mind is the core from which all else comes from. Where you go next is all in your heard.

Equally, what will stop you is also in your head. Not to discount the fact that there are some real and tangible obstacles, but your mind gets to decide what those obstacles mean to you. Your mind has the power to increase or to shrink any presented obstacles. Your mind has the power to see beyond barriers. Also, your mind gets to decide to break through barriers.

So, you can sit still and contemplate life and function with what life has handed you or you can take what life has granted you and make something of it, which could leverage you to move to the next level. This is how you turn the page. Those obstacles are gifts. When we go against them, we get to learn what we are made of. We get to test and develop new levels of strength.

How to choose to rise in the midst of challenges is the shaping tool that makes you fit for the future.

Many of us don't like change, yet the only thing that is constant in our life is change. A true leader and manager of their own life-brand understand and embraces change. We cut our teeth on change. We know that if we master change, we have that edge that gets us ahead of many. We get to do something outside of the norm. Obstacle and change are not our enemies. They are our teacher. They give us the customized life lessons we so badly need.

Easy is not a part of our diet. We hunger for the life of change. We know that the diet of change is what will help us to grow into full maturity and to rightly fulfill our role in life.

We don't back down. We bear down and move ahead. Taking ground, inch-by-inch. We move with a sense of belief of what is to come. We anticipate what is on the next page. But to us, it is a blank page that we get to write. We get to write our own story. We align ourselves with our called-out future. We become resourceful and excited about what we will bring to fruition. So, come on future!! We are ready for you!!

Positive Affirmation:
Don't let fear of failure pin you down. The battle is not won by laying on your belly. Get up and fight. Stay committed to winning or die trying.

Self-Assessment Questions:

- What are some core things you hope to engage in, in the very near future?
- What role do you see yourself playing in that future?
- What examples of failure-to-success stories do you have before you?
- How much weight does your past have in reflection to your future?
- How have you trained yourself to overcome y our past?
- Who is within your circle of success?
- Who should you weed out of your circle of success?
- How have you been encouraged to transform obstacles into learning opportunities?
- To what degree have you installed assurance that you are on the right path for yourself?
- Are you true to your path? Have you done your honest best up until now? Is there room for growth? What steps will you take today?
- Is there a high level of passion associated with the thing that you are pursuing?
- What old methods are you still using to reach your new goals? Do you need to change any of your methods?
- What is your quitting point? What do you need to tell yourself in order to get you to quit quitting?

Branded and Bold Quotes:

- "Sometimes people with the worst pasts end up creating the best futures."
- "I stopped explain myself when I realized people only understand from their level of perception."
- "The impediment to action is action. What stands in the way becomes the way." – Marcus Aurelius
- "If you are facing in the right direction, all you need to do is keep walking." – Buddha
- "Good things come to those who wait, but better things come to those who work for it."
- "Always go with your passions. Never ask yourself if it's realistic or not." - Deepak Chopra
- "Every time you are tempted to react in the same old way, ask if you want to be a prisoner of the past or a pioneer of the future." – Deepak Chopra
- "Continuous effort – not strength or intelligence – is the key to unlocking our potential." – Winston Churchill
- Happiness lies in the joy of achievement and the thrill of creative effort." – Franklin D. Roosevelt
- "Inhale the future, exhale the past."

Action Steps:
Make a list of all your obstacles. Line then up and execute them one-by-one. Become relentless in pursuit in who you MUST become. Do not deny yourself.

DAY 13 - WAKE UP DETERMINED...

Imagine for a moment, what it feels like to be bullied. Someone in your face every day, tormenting you. Hunting you down and not allowing you a moment of peace. You cringe whenever in their presence. This person words come out at you like a sledgehammer cracking against your bones. Breaking you daily, to a new degree. Their expression makes you contemplate death. Giving you the desire to give up.

Now imagine when you were at your lowest moment, someone whispers to you, "if you want the attacks to stop, stand up to your bully." You take it lightly at first, but after a while, you get a level of assurance to the possibility of that statement. You start to believe in your heart-of-hearts that you actually do have a shot at putting an end to all this harassment.

So you spend the next few days getting pumped for your encounter. You metaphorically start pumping iron and shadow boxing. You give yourself that pep talk of determination. You tell yourself you will not settle for defeat. You get that newfound determination to finally face your Goliaths.

You spend the weekend giving that final prayer, saying it is now or never. There is no turning back. Sunday night comes, and you get ready to rest, but you are anxious. You know that tomorrow, it ends, one way or another. So you sleep, but your mind is racing. Contemplating the possibilities.

The alarm rings, and that's the signal. You wake up with determination. You get ready, and you head to the old familiar place where you would get bullied. "NO MORE!" you say. I will not back down. I will not surrender. Instead of hiding from your bully, you go and find him. You walk into his space and get eye to eye, and you declare that it ends today. The bully, feeling surprised but yet still confident that he could take you comes at you. But you, preparing for this, choose to stand your ground and you go for it. Determined to take your self-respect back. Hits are exchanged, and the fight only last for a moment, but seemed like an eternity, comes to an end.

In this moment of imagination, what I failed to mention was that the bully you had been facing all along has been yourself. Your doubts, fears, past failures, hurts, and the stories that went along with them. Today is the day you take action. Today is the day you face your giants. Today you stop with the stories of why is life happening to me, and you start asking how you can do something about it.

You see, when you had to look the bully eye-to-eye, you were looking in a mirror. You got to see the weakness of the stories you have been telling yourself. Time to stop the bullying and stand up for yourself. Decide to makes some changes in y our life. Develop a new determination. Declare a renewed belief in yourself.

The only thing standing between you and the life you want is yourself. What are you willing to do in order to get yourself out of your own way?

Get up in your own face and go toe-to-toe. Don't accept mediocrity. Be determined to be more today, than you were yesterday.

All it takes to win is the determination to stay in the fight longer than you anticipated. So, resolve never to give up, until you have won. The victory is at hand. Are you willing to reach for it?

Positive Affirmation:
Be real and welcome opposition. Oppositions are only opportunities to increase your strength. We grow through perseverance.

Self-Assessment Questions:

- What will total satisfaction look like once you hit your goals?
- Are you willing to fail? How do you define failure? In what way can a failure shape you?
- How do you measure or define success?
- When you fail do you still find yourself moving forward?
- What steps are you taking today that feed into the results you hope to get tomorrow?
- How do you speak to yourself when facing an opposition?
- What are some core reminders of success and perseverance you use to help you when you are in a rut?

- How high are your expectations for yourself when it comes to your personal development?
- Who would you most likely want to model your life after?
- What are the things that you are currently engaged in that conflict with what you want for your future? Can you take a stance and stop any of it now?
- Have you ever beaten yourself up for not taking action? How did that help your situation or move you forward?

Branded and Bold Quotes:

- "Wake up with determination. Go to bed with satisfaction."
- "Success is going from failure to failure with no loss of enthusiasm." – Winston Churchill
- "Just because it's not happening right now, doesn't mean it never will."
- "What you think, you become. What you feel, you attract. What you imagine, you create." – Buddha
- "An awake heart is like a sky that pours light."
- "You can suffer the pain of change or suffer remaining the way you are." – Joyce Meyer
- "Attract what you expect, reflect what you desire, become what you respect, mirror what you admire."
- "The reason people awaken is that they have finally stopped agreeing to things that insult their soul."
- "No matter how you feel, get up, dress up, show up, and never give up!"
- "Don't be afraid to fail, be afraid not to try."

Action Steps:
Close your eyes (Metaphorically). Now visualize with your heart. Go beyond the limitations of your mind. Connect your imagination with your determination and grid. Now open your eyes and make it happen.

DAY 14 - INVITING VISION

What if someone were to come to you and say that in a far-off land, there was a king, that was ill, but trusted members of his cabinet had to keep it secret that he was ill or else the country would go into pure chaos. They approached you because you had a strong likeness to the king, but they asked if you could stand in for a short while, while the king recovered.

However, in order to assume the role you had to learn his mannerisms, walk, and talk. You had to learn how to fit into his role. You needed to learn all of his habits so that you could pass flawlessly. You consent in order to keep peace in that county.

However, your reservation was that you could not measure up. So, you go to work on yourself. You look at pictures and watch videos of the king. You practice for hours. You find it difficult because there are accents and language barriers. But you stay true to the model of the king. Why? Because as you studied the king, you find that he was a great man that loved and cared for his people. You didn't want to let him or his people down.

His team sneaks you into the country under the cover of darkness. They take you to the royal palace, where you complete your rehearsal. Then the day comes. Time for you to pass the test. They send you before a crowd in a royal ceremony to deliver a speech. You are nervous, but you stand and deliver flawlessly. You own the part, and the people are none the wiser. A sense of comfort and confidence sets in due to your level of achievement. You not only acted the part. You became the part. You owned it with deep conviction.

Now move from your imagination onto your life stage. There is a calling upon your life. A role you have been asked to play. It requires for you to study a script and become the part. Own the vision, if you will, of the person you are to become.

In a sense, you are real, and you have been granted a kingdom to lead. That kingdom is your life. Your subjects are your emotions, feeling, will, desires, and hopes. They need you to lead and nurture them to fulfill the role. Will you let your country fall into darkness and chaos because you have not yet stepped up to your vision?

Take some time to really study your part. Get a really good idea of who you were called to be. Do you see it clearly yet? Focus. Go to work and practice. Own it. Soon you will be called to the center stage of your own life. Will you be ready for your life's performance?

> **Positive Affirmation:**
> You are only limited by your own beliefs. Your actions reveal your real beliefs. Take actions that match what you want.

Self-Assessment Questions:

- Have you ever made a mistake?
- How have you been conditioned to interpret mistakes?
- What are the most valuable lessons you have learned from your mistakes?
- What helps your focus on your vision?
- What risk are you apprehensive about taking?
- What does risk mean to you?
- What risk in the past have you taken where you experienced any form of success?
- Where do you spend the bulk of your time?
- Do you feel that your time committal reveal what your true vision may be?
- Check your attitude: What does your attitude attract and what direction is it setting for you?
- How creative are you with the future you are shaping?
- What goals or activity continually haunt your mind? Are you putting any real action toward any of it?

- Has fear every limited any changes you have been wanting to make in your life?
- Does fear dominate or limit your life choices?
- Has fear or failure crippled you to the point where you don't want to get out of bed?
- How much of your failed past are you trying to drag into your future?
- Are any of your failures toxic to your current existence?
- Have you designed a future that shock you to the point where you are so excited that you can't stop working on it?
- What area of faith do you need to pour into your plan for future so that it can crush your fears?

Branded and Bold Quotes:

- "Don't place mistakes on your head; their weight may crush you. Instead, place them under your feet and use them as a platform to view your horizons."
- "Hold the vision, trust the process."
- "Only those who will risk going too far can possibly find out how far they can go." – T. S. Elliot
- "Focus your best hours on your biggest opportunities." – Robin Sharma
- "Your attitude determines your direction."
- "The best way to predict the future is to create it."
- "If you can't stop thinking about it, don't stop working for it."
- "Don't be afraid of change. It is leading you to a new beginning."

- "You can't start the next chapter of your life if you keep re-reading the last one."
- "Create a vision that makes you wanna jump out of bed in the morning."
- "Make your vision so clear that your fears become irrelevant."

> **Action Steps:**
> **Get clear in your head what you want. Get solid in the steps it takes to get there. Dismiss your fears. Do at least one thing today that agrees with your vision.**

WEEK 3 – ARISE

Bold Declaration #3 - **ARISE:** I will **ARISE** and engage life at its highest level.

Let's recap. So far, in week 1, we took a brief overview of our DREAMS. The ultimate gift. If anybody ever gave you a gift, and it is the best tangible gift you could ever receive, it would struggle with the gift of a dream. A dream has the power to stir the emotions and can cause you to take action. We got to review the question: What are the possibilities? Why we dream and how to dream and especially what our dreams mean to us today and tomorrow. We discovered that our dreams are our mental playground where we get to play with the possibilities. A treasure of eternal value. We discover our own personal values, and we got to challenge our core beliefs. I hope you have been actively engaging in the pursuit of your dreams.

In week 2, we moved to the AWAKE phase. This is

where you hear the buzz. This is that moment where you get the shove. That event that moves you out of that passive dreaming state to the point of examining your realities. In this section, we explored the question: Where am I? We got to look at our station in life. This state raised a lot of questions. You got to look at what you've been doing with your life. You got to examine the plan you have been operating under. Questioning if that plan is good enough or is there more you should or could be doing? We got to review what is governing your life, and you got to discover WHO MUST govern your life.

If you have been following along, you will have discovered; this book is for those, who are mature enough to see that throughout much of society, there has been many who are around us but have been asleep and just going through the motions. This guide is designed to put you into action. I hoped you get antsy and stirred to get up and do something. If you looked in the mirror and did not like what you see, I want you to get mad. Mad enough to change what you don't like seeing every day.

Now, let's go to work. I am about to move you out the bed and get you engaged. There is so much life to live and today is the day you start living. In week 3. We ARISE. We explored the question: When is now? The question in itself does not make sense. But if you take a moment and step outside of yourself and examine the ridiculousness of this question you will see that we have abused the clock. A clock is a tool designed to measure time. Like sands that drip down in an hourglass, once it goes down in a given moment, it does not naturally rise. That moment has past will never be seen again. We can either use moments or get used by our moments.

In this section, you will be encouraged to remove all excused for what you have not been living and engaging in life. You only get one. You have been grated so much when it comes to time and ability. Don't waste another minute. Don't let another second go by without you doing at least one thing to fulfill your life's calling.

It doesn't matter if you are in a hospital bed, wheelchair, in prison, or in a dead-end job you feel that you hate. This is getting real and getting past blame and moving to a level of life that holds you highly accountable for its outcome. No more blaming others for what happens in your life. Take action and responsibility and rise and shape your future.

Move past thinking about it and being a perpetual student. You have studied it long enough. Today is the day you commit to action. No more hitting that snooze button. There is nothing left in that bed. Get up and go live. Go discover. Go build. The world is sick, and you are the medicine. But the world will never get the cure until you rise and show up. So wipe the sleep from your eyes. Shake your body out. Give it a good stretch, and it's now time to start moving. We have a lot of work today. Turn the page and meet me. This is going to be a challenging but yet a fun week. Let's get to it!

DAY 15 - DROP WEIGHT

When a boxer trains for a match and when they find themselves overweight, he has to go through some rigorous training in order to right-size their body so they can be in range to qualify for the match. They not only have to train to lose weight, but they also have to train in speed, strength, stamina, and strategies. In order to get ready, there is a level of sacrifice that must be made, and much of it is tied to a period of short-term pain in order to lead to long-term gains in the ring.

But, if a fighter loses focus and chooses to cut corners, they could find themselves outmatched and out-gunned, and the fight could take a lot out of him. So, there has to be a commitment to excellence, and they have to come to terms with any non-productive habits and behavior. In order to experience success, those behaviors must be put to rest. They don't serve, and in many cases, they lead to a limited future.

A fighter has to get real with themselves. In a way, they have to make an agreement with pain. You see, pain is a very powerful teaching. The word, itself, has a negative connotation, but in fact, many of the greatest things that this world has ever produced has come to a certain level of pain. We, humans, are moved by either a massive amount of pleasure or a massive amount of pain. How we interpret what pleasure and pain mean determine our direction and pace that we'll move.

So, have you examined where your life is headed? Have you taken some time to look at your habits, beliefs, and practices in how they contribute to what you're getting out of life? Looking back, have you looked at how those habits have shaped you into what you are experiencing today? What if you never adjusted, how would your habits or beliefs impact the type of life you really wanted? If you had a chance to change your habits, what would you modify? How could those changes move you to a better place that is more appealing? Will there be a struggle that makes you uncomfortable enough to make those changes? If you could tolerate the pain of the changes you needed to make, what positive outcome could you achieve?

Those are some deep questions, but they are powerful in how they can move you to a place that matches your true desire. As you look at your life-brand, think about what it will take to mold it. It won't be easy, but it will be worth it.

Positive Affirmation:
Commit to daily letting go of things that are not moving you toward your goals.

Self-Assessment Questions:

- I have experienced roadblocks from the following every time I attempted to pursue my goals…..?
- Do you blame anyone or any events for you not hitting your goals?
- If I sent more time on the following, I could get traction on hitting my goals….?
- The following habits have aided me with getting closer to my goals….?
- The following habits have halted me from getting closer to my goals….?
- The following habit, if I improve would dramatically move me closer to success…..?
- How strong are your beliefs with aiding you toward hitting your mark?
- This is what I see when I visualize my own personal success…..?
- If I remain on this current life course, I will end up doing the following….?
- I am committed to making the following sacrifices in order to reach my goals….?
- What is your long-term pleasure and how will you get to this?
- How do you use the information that your emotions give you with determining your path?
- What lessons have you learned from watching others experience?
- How has pain or pleasure motivated you in the past with getting things done for your greater good?

- What is the root of my limiting thinking? Why am I allowing it to continue? What has it cost me?
- How has my unhelpful behavior benefited me? How will my new habits be equally powerful with supporting me?
- How has this new behavior promoted growth and contribution?
- How will you support your new positive change?
- How will you monitor and manage your newly changed behavior?
- How can you preemptive your potential failures?

Branded and Bold Quotes:

- "Don't put in ½ of the effort unless you're okay with ½ of the results."
- "Be stronger than excuses"
- "Always be a first-rate version of yourself, instead of a second-rate of somebody else." – Judy Garland
- "Starting today, I need to forget what's gone. Appreciate what still remains and look forward to what's coming next."
- "In the end, we only regret the chances we didn't take, the relationship we are afraid to have, and the decisions we waited too long to make."
- "Falling down is an accident. Staying down is a choice."
- "The strongest people aren't always the people who win, but the people who don't give up when they lose."
- "Your body can stand almost anything. It's your mind that you have to convince."

- "Working hard for something we don't care about is called stress. Working hard for something we love is called passion."
- "Be somebody nobody thought you could be."

> **Action Steps:**
> **Identify the most detrimental habit that you have and tell someone about it and ask for help with addressing it**

DAY 16 - TAKE A NEW PATH

You have come to fork in the road. You were on a single path that has now become two. Which way to go? Does it matter what path? Is one good and one bad? Life demands a decision at all times. There are those that hate being placed in a position of having to make a decision. However, to not make a decision is a decision in itself. We don't get to clock out.

So, what's a person to do? If you have to make a decision why not make it fit? Fit what? You may ask. The best fit is to anchor your decision to a goal. Not so much to an outcome, but to a direction. You see, we, can set goals and press hard to reach them, but miss the most important part about pursuing the goal. That is, we need to look at who we are becoming as we travel the path.

The goal, in so many cases, is secondary. The goal is a temporary placeholder designed to get us moving. We, creatures, thrive the best when we are in motion. When we sit still too long, then we become stagnate and lulled to sleep, and we miss out on the treasures of life. But to move, we have to decide to move. We have to set goals and seek out paths that best match up to those goals.

We have to also review what all is required to travel the selected path. It may require an education. It may require help from friends, finances, faith, and fervor. Whatever it is, it takes a good accounting and passion to ask lots of really great questions. Along with those choices, you have to consider a variation to those choices and define any potential roadblocks along with the most appropriate response to anything that could hinder your journey.

You also have to define what success to you is or what your expectation is. This serves as motivation to keep moving forward. If you can recognize signs of life, then your activation factors will climb higher and inspire you to keep going and growing. Along with resources and goal definition, you need to come up with a series of waypoints. Places along your journey where you can stop, regroup and assess your progress.

Instead of going after one big win, you can develop momentum by nailing a series of short wins. But no matter what, see yourself and a champion. Visualize what you want and how you will get there. See yourself slicing through the opposition. Own your journey. Become relentless in your pursuit. Think about it so much that you could describe it in detail and could recognize it when it shows up in your face. This will cause your feet to move in the right direction. But above all, don't forget to capture the main thing. Examine who you become along the journey. Deicide today!!!

> **Positive Affirmation:**
> **The goal is not the goal. The goal just gets you on the path of discovery.**

Self-Assessment Questions:

- When it comes to tough decisions, what method do you use to make up your mind?
- What key goals have you hit in the past?
- How important are your goals for you?
- How did it make you feel that you met your goal?
- What discoveries did you make about yourself as a result of reaching your goals?
- How have your goals shaped your character and your outlook?
- Do you feel your limitations barriers have expanded since you started hitting your goals?
- How resourceful would you consider yourself?
- To what length would you go in order to hit your goals?
- Where is the point you will stop when it comes to your goals?

Branded and Bold Quotes:

> "Sometimes you face difficulties not because you're doing something wrong, but because you're doing something right."
> "Start today; I need to forget what's gone. Appreciate what still remains and look forward to what's coming next."

- "Do not follow the path may lead go instead where there is no path and leave a trail."
- "Two things prevent us from happiness; living in the past and observing others."
- "Everything is going to be OK in the end. If it is not OK, it's not the end."
- "It is never too late to be what you might have been." – George Eliot
- "The key to realizing a dream is to focus not on success, but the significance and then even the small steps and little victories along your path will take on greater meaning." – Oprah
- "I'm not here to be average; I'm here to be awesome."
- "At any given moment you have the power to say: This is not how the story is going to end."
- "Set a goal to achieve something that is so big, so exhilarating that it excites you and scares you at the same time." – Bob Proctor

> **Action Steps:**
> **Along with setting goals take some time to detail the steps from where you are to where you want to be.**

DAY 17 - GET UP!

You've been taunted long enough. Teased by your dreams of what could be. Enticed into believing that this could be yours. You awoke from your dream and contemplated the possibilities. Is this for real? How is it possible that I can do this? I have never done anything like this before. Your experience starts to chime in. You take inventory of your failures. Your newfound faith starts to shrink. You question the possibilities. And you lay there. Paralyzed by your own fears.

As sick as it sounds, here is the cold hard, honest truth. If you lay there and do nothing, eventually the better part of you will for certain. But if you want to live, I mean really live, it comes from taking actions. So, pull, push, reach, climb, scream and ask for help, but you got to get up out of your bed of disease. You got to move. Don't think. Move! Don't analyze, contemplate, review options, or examine. Get out of your head and get out of bed.

It's time for some wild, crazy, massive action. Move as if your bed was on fire and you are trying to save your own life. Go after your destiny. Take raw, unadulterated, committed action. That's what true responsibility really us. No excuses. Just action. You got to get resourceful and abandon all excuses. Refuse to settle until you reached your dreams.

It's time to get uncomfortable with your moves toward success. You can't outsource the work. You got to get up for yourself. You got to move past the thought and move into pure action.

Now as you move, fear-chatter will spike up, but here is what you do with this chatter. Say SO WHAT!?!? So what, if you fail, then you are in good company. You can't get to greatness unless you are willing to fail. Perfect is an illusion. Perfection is what we are really after. The never-ending attitude to be better than you were yesterday. No one else can be responsible for the motion or the direction you are taking. That is purely up to you. In our navigation of life and our desire to get up and get into it, we must understand, that life is a series of problems. We must approach it in this way so we can have the right expectation.

True growth and maturity take place when we understand that we learn how to master the problems. Once you move to that stage, you will never be lulled to sleep again.

Positive Affirmation:
Say "SO WHAT!?!?" So what, if you fail, then you are in good company.

Self-Assessment Questions:

- What have you been holding back on take action on?
- What's the worst that could happen if you don't take action?

- What's the best if you do take action?
- Do you use L.U.C.K. (Living Under Correct Knowledge)?
- What things have you been resourceful in the past when it comes to solving complexed life problems?
- Do you ever find yourself hesitating on your decision?
- How has this helped or hindered the outcome?
- Do you own or rent your decisions?
- If you are not driving your own decisions, then why not?
- Life is a series of problems – What are you doing daily to find new ways to master problems?

Branded and Bold Quotes:

- "When everything feels like an uphill struggle, just think of the view from the top."
- "Here's what I think integrity is: It's choosing courage over comfort. Choosing what's right over what's fun, fast or easy, and practice your values." – Brene Brown
- "Life has no remote, get up and change it yourself."
- "Nothing holds you back more than your own insecurities."
- "Great things never came from comfort zones."
- "Your attitude determines your direction."
- "The fact that you aren't where you want to be should be enough motivation."
- "To accomplish great things, we must not only act but also dream, not only plan but also believe." – Anatole France

- "Let no one discourage your ambitious attitude. You don't need a fan club to achieve your goals. Be your own motivation." – Mama Zara
- "Surround yourself with people who have dreams, desire, and ambition; they'll help you push for, and realize your own."

> **Action Steps:**
> **Find something that you attempted recently that you failed at and give it another try.**

DAY 18 - BETTER THAN YESTERDAY

Close your eyes. Take a moment to breathe. Slow things down a bit. Now set your focus on tomorrow. Not just any tomorrow, but the one that was tailored made for you. One where everything went perfectly. You got up on time. You had the right frame of mind. You were happy and excited. You went to the mirror and did your power affirmation. You declared that you were a winner. Then you took action. Raw, unfiltered action on building your perfect day. You were focused and fixed. You listed the required resources to get a thing done and you summoned them, one by one, and as obstacles popped up, they were quickly mowed down. The goals you set, we're getting done. Your motivational energy was booted to its maximum level. You walked through your day, feeling good that you worked hard, got a lot done, blessed a lot of people through your efforts and you used that day as a positive stepping stone that moved you closer to your goals.

Now open your eyes. It's time to go to work on building that day. In your dream life, things will go smooth. In reality, you will encounter problems. You may even repeat some problems from yesterday. But I have to ask, "Did you learn something?" What did your mistakes and failures teach you? If you have repeated the same mistakes or set back more than once, then you may need to start there before moving forward. A person who is really in tuned with mastering their life brand is connected with their limitation, and they know how to go to work on it. If you can repeat and locate what is broken, you are then one more step closer to eliminating that sequence from your life flow. Serve notice to your habitual problem and commit to locate and eliminate them. Once you know your limit, then you can find the right resources to use to break past them.

Ultimately, the intent here is to help you see that most limitation will be directly associated with habits that you have. If you can alter your habits, then you can alter your future. If you have in your habit, a lot of distractions, then I can guarantee that you are not putting any real work on things associate to your goals. You see, most of our goals have some level of discomfort to it. So, we use a distraction to avoid pain. So we numb ourselves with a distraction that keeps us active, but not productive. So, look at what you engage in. Ask, "Is it serving my stated goals?

As you make changes and move along your path of life, one valuable lesson I would like to share is that it's not about the goal as much as it is about who we become along the journey. It's great to hit our goals, but it's more fulfilling to understand the transformation we went through in order to reach that goal.

Lastly, what has prevented most changes for a better life is the willingness never to fail. However, if you're willing never to fail, then you also have to be comfortable with never achieving. The best of many great ideas come through repeated failures. Failures are our classroom. Enter in, every day and learn something. Your failures will take you on a journey beyond your wildest imagination. Fall in love with failures - Failure is feedback and fuel for future development.

> **Positive Affirmation:**
> **Once you know your limit, then you can find the right resources to use to break past them.**

Self-Assessment Questions:

- How have the stories of your youth impacted how you function today?
- On a scale from 1 to 10 where 10 is very important, how important is it for you to have a totally comfortable life?
- Why is comfort so important to you?
- Things that are of value to you did any of that come through comfort or work?
- What was the toughest thing you had to endure in order to achieve something great?
- Has pain, pressure, trials ever been a motivating factor in any of your thought process?
- What are some of the greatest life lessons that your mistakes and failures have taught you?
- Do you view your limitation as permanent or temporary?

- When you are working on your goals do you ever find it hard to get things done due to distractions?
- Do you assess how you spend time on things that are not related to reaching your goals?
- What are some of the things you could give up or put on hold for a season while you work on hitting your goals?
- As you have traveled this far on this journey, have you noticed any major shift in your personality?
- Who did you become today?
- How cool are with failing?
- What does failure mean to you?
- Are you willing to fall in love with failure?
- Do you view it as data that you could use to improve your personal product that you offer to the world?

Branded and Bold Quotes:

- "It's not about being the best. It's about being better than you were yesterday."
- "Almost every successful person begins with two beliefs: the future can be better than the present, and I have the make it so"
- "My dreams are my dress rehearsals for my future." – David Copperfield
- "The only person you should try to be better than…is the person you were yesterday."
- "Things that excite you are not random. They are connected to your purpose. Follow them."
- "Never believe that a few caring people can't change the world. For, indeed, that's all whoever have." – Margret Mead

> "The past is your lesson. The present is your gift. The future is your motivation."
> "A great attitude becomes a great day which becomes a great month which becomes a great year which becomes a great life." – Mandy Hale
> "You must learn to master a new way to think before you can master a new way to be." – Marianne Williamson
> "Your focus determines your reality."

Action Steps:
Commit to not watching TV or going on social media while you spend an entire day working on your goals.

DAY 19 - TIME TO DEVELOP

When it comes to your life or career, in order to enhance it, it requires some form of growth. This is sometimes called personal development (PD). It is something you hear people talk about at times, but to be clear, it is something that is addressed at a personal level. When you are the CEO of your life and are managing your brand well, when you develop, you don't do it for window dressing so you can look good on the outside. This is something that hits at the core and transforms from the inside out.

A target drives your development. If you have not gotten clear on what you want, then you will leave a lot of room for distractions to pop up with no recourse. PD is to move expeditiously toward a goal with full intentionality. Each person will be different in their target and pursuit of happiness. The enabler is habit management. A professional life brand manager will take daily inventory of their habits and assess what is moving them toward or away from their goals. They then will perform habit acquisitions. They will locate and emulate other high-end achievers and monitor their habits and look for things to emulate. They also look for habits to eliminate.

You can look at it as if there was a square peg that needed to fit into a square hole. If that peg didn't fit, the creator would whittle away segments until they got it just right so it could fit. We can view the whole as our true calling and whittle pieces are habits that are non-conducive to who we are supposed to be in the future. So, we make new choices to go to new places.

Personal development does not necessarily lead us to success. However, it has the power to help us understand what success really means to us, and it moves us to a place where we can feel fulfilled each and every day of the journey. It helps us understand our WHY, and it encourages us to get our mind, body, soul, in sync to who we are and what we were meant to be and governs the action we take and measure we use to determine if we are working to the right blueprint for our future.

DP is not easy, and it is not for the faint of heart. It will make you mad or at the least, uncomfortable. Meaningful change that comes easy is an illusion. True change will take you to places that will stretch you. Therefore you have to commit to partner with discomfort. For, the best changes will come through the challenges we were willing to face. Understand that with this challenge will come a series of failures. Let your failures become your classroom when you get to come and ask questions. Failures are not be feared but embraced. Failures give you answers about yourself and limitation. It gives a list of things to work on and resources to gather. If you can adjust your attitude and views on failures, this will give you the power and trajectory you need to move into the person you were ultimately destined to become.

> **Positive Affirmation:**
> **Personal development is to move expeditiously toward a goal with full intentionality.**

Self-Assessment Questions:

- What does a life live on purpose look like?
- Do you know any high-end performers?
- Who would you most like to pattern your life after?
- What are some of the rough edges that you need to chisel away at in your life and habits?
- What does it mean to live a full and intentional life?
- How does the way you define success impact how you feel about yourself today?
- Do your words, thoughts, and action all sync up? How does it feel when they are not?
- Are you willing to partner with discomfort for the greater good? What does that look like to you?
- In what ways do you invest in yourself, daily?
- You can't outsource your life, but what areas can you outsource so you can get to manage the main thing?
-

Branded and Bold Quotes:

- "Stop hating yourself for everything you aren't and start loving yourself for everything you already are."
- "Never dream of success but work for it."
- "Sometimes God calms the storm. Sometimes God calms the sailor. But sometimes he makes us swim."
- "Never give up on a dream just because of the time it will take to accomplish it. The time will pass away anyway." – Earl Nightingale
- "Life loves to be taken by the lapel and told, 'I'm with you, kid. Let's go.' " – Maya Angelou
- "By constant self-discipline and self-control, you can develop greatness of character." – Grenville Kleiser
- "If you don't challenge yourself, you will never realize what you can become."
- "Only those who will risk going too far can possibly find out how far one can go." – T.S. Eliot
- "Stop being afraid of what could go wrong, and focus on what could go right."
- "You don't get rid of yesterday by talking about it all the time; you get rid of its effect on you by moving forward."

Action Steps:
Make a list of 5 people you would most like to pattern your life after and seek out their winning habits.

DAY 20 - THIS IS GOING TO HURT

Who in their right mind loves pain? Not too many people. Pain can cause you to rethink what you are doing. Past pains can stick with you and can shape your future choices. Pain also has the power to move you. If under enough pressure and pain, a person can be moved to perform acts that are way outside of their norm. Pain reveals the barriers that are in our lives that keep us from our prescribed vision. That barrier stands between us and the very thing we have never had but knows in our heart-of-hearts that which we really want. But in order to get there, we must press in and go through. As we stay focused and fixed on our goals and we continue to press we start to learn some things about ourselves. We not only learn that we don't like pain, but we get to find our points where we could break down. But those same points are areas we get to do some focused work, to sure-up so we can face the next round of events. That's the cool think about being humans. We get to reason and analyze. We get to develop and improve.

There is power in excitement. Not only are we granted a vision of what's to come in our personal transformation, we also have the option to get excited about the outcome. The more we allow ourselves to celebrate what's to come, the more energy we will have to press within on our development. Pain is a false prison. Constructed by suggestions from our past failures and that of others. These are a false limitation that persuades us to be OK with being comfortable. It encourages us to check out and chill. We will make up a story to justify our lack of action which will make it OK to resort to fatalism. That dreaded story that failure is a part of our history and destiny. How cruel is that? In life, we are either going to be tempted or tested. Tempting will persuade you to give up and give into the easy and live to a limit. Testing will take us layer by layer to higher heights. All it takes is a simple shift in order to realize the full potential and possibilities of your implanted vision.

Distractions and pain go hand-in-hand. Change requires action. Change requires commitment and determination. But a change in many cases requires discomfort. There are many great things in store for our lives on the other side of pain. However, most people would prefer to numb themselves so not to experience pain. We get upset and depressed. We tell stores and seek therapy. This may reveal a problem, but we come to a conclusion that life is not fare. So do we holler foul? No, we address our judgments on the situation, and we fight for justice, and we fight to right the scales of life. One of the most effective ways to balance the scales of life is to develop at the personal level. It takes the control out of others hands and places the responsibility right where it belongs. In your own hands.

Identify your path and pain. Measure the cost and press through to discover the new you. Pain will not last always, and it may endure for the night, but joy will come in the morning.

> **Positive Affirmation:**
> **Be OK with pain. Growth comes from it.**

Self-Assessment Questions:

- What would you say are your top 5 strengths?
- What areas would you say you need to develop?
- Have you put an honest effort in the past into addressing your developmental issues?
- Do you value what you are learning about yourself?
- How does it make you feel to link power to your pain and frustration?
- What are some limiting beliefs from your past that has stopped you from taking action?
- Do you think fear is powerful enough to cancel out your future?
- What helps you to focus on the things you need to change?
- What limits have your past pain revealed to you?
- What strategies have you developed to address these limits?

Branded and Bold Quotes:

> "Believe in yourself and all that you are. Know that there is something inside you that is greater than any obstacle." – Christian Larson

- "The struggle of life is one of our greatest blessings. It makes us patient, sensitive, and godlike. It teaches us that although the world is full of suffering, it is also full of the overcoming of it." _ Helen Keller
- "Wanting something is not enough. You must hunger for it. Your motivation must be absolutely compelling in order to overcome the obstacles that will invariably come your way." – Les Brown
- "Life will beat you up a lot, so be proud of each and every trial you came through. The physical and emotional scars of those trials are medals of bravery for not giving up."
- "The best way out is always through." – Robert Frost
- "The darkest night produce the brightest stars."
- "The struggle you're in today is developing the strength you need for tomorrow."
- "Do what you got to do so can do what you wanna do." – Denzel Washington
- "Never let a stumble be the end of your journey."
- "Good timber does not grow with ease. The stronger the wind, the stronger the trees." – Thomas S. Monson

---

Action Steps:
Commit through the pain and attempt again on something that failed that brought discomfort. Find victory on the other side.

DAY 21 - RESPONSE-ABLE

When managing your life and shaping your destiny, how empowered do you feel that you can shape and firm the desired outcome? As you ponder this question, do so while reflecting on the ownership of your life up till now. Give credit to your parents if they played an active role in helping structure an initial life plan. Not all of us have that option and if you did, stop right now and go give your supporter a call, send them a card or give them a hug. At the least, send warm thoughts of them up into the atmosphere, for they are true stars.

Along with the shaping of your life requires power. In this teaching, I am promotion self-mastery and in this case, setting a high understanding and expectation of responsibility. Responsibility is a standard of actions that measures your progress toward a goal, or it may reveal that you either have no goals or are not actively working on them. It's the ability to respond to events, people, and statements in a way that constantly moves you toward your goal.

Mastery of this requires focus and commitment, the level of commitment to be completely honest with oneself. Examining who you were, what you are, and what you hope to be. A truly responsible person is outcome driven. Situations or people do not handle them. But they manage their emotional response in a way that it directs feelings and events and orders them to get in sync with the expected future and outcome.

A responsible person is always on. They anticipate and engage life in such a way that they promote others to understand and to work toward similar actions that support their outcome. Responsible life-Brand managers don't look for or make excuses. They seek truth in themselves and fight for a higher response. They admit mistakes and are committed to a solution. They don't bow or bend to circumstance. They know that the more they take action, the more power they add to their ability to respond.

They garnered respect at the highest level because their acts of responsibility speak for themselves. They are the managers of their constant dwelling thought. Leaving none to be stray, but focusing them with the intent to promote a progressive outcome. Responsible leaders don't use the escape clause where when things are unpleasant and not going their way; they don't bail or sabotage any progress.

A responsible person clamps down and holds on because they are committed to the hopeful outcome and will seek out resources and adjust to promote that said outcome. Responsibility is internal and self-centered in the sense that if there is a problem, then a responsible person admits and takes action. They never seek to put anything on anyone else until they have openly and honestly addressed their role in any failure. Also, the efforts of success rest with and go to the responsible person as well.

As a parameter, if you ever find yourself irritated, frustrated, angered, egotistical, arrogant, or in defense of something, there is an underlining tone that may indicate that there is an area of your life you have not taken the right honest action in association to a particular event. If you find yourself talking about what you are going to do way more than the affiliated action, then you may not be taking responsibility either.

> **Positive Affirmation:**
> **If you are thinking about or talking about it more than taking action on it, then you are not being responsible.**

Self-Assessment Questions:

- I have taken the following steps in the past 24 hours that helped moved me closer to my goals….?
- Are there people you can blame for promoting your failures?
- Are there people you can thank for assisting you with your success?
- The following are my known common distractions from taking action….?
- I appreciate and want to emulate the following people and their habits….?
- I find that these common reoccurring thoughts feed into the habits that I practice….?

- The following people influence my motivations and ability to be responsible....?
- I find myself irritated when I expect actions in the following area....?
- I irritations reveal the following about my role of responsibility to any give situation...?
- I find myself talking about a situation more than taking action, and it caused me to feel the following...?
- What emotions do I want to project more and what emotions do want to encounter?
- How have things that I have learned lately influenced my level of decisions and responses?
- How are your angered responses when it comes to newly discovered truths?

Branded and Bold Quotes:

- "As we arise each morning let us determine to respond with more love and kindness to whatever might come our way." – Thomas S. Monson
- "The more that you read, the more things you will know. The more that you learn, the more places you'll go. – Dr. Seuss
- "The greatest weapon against stress is our ability to choose one thought over another." – William James
- "Life is not about waiting for the storm to pass but learning to dance in the rain."
- "She stood in the storm, and when the wind did not blow her way, she adjusted her sails." – Elizabeth Edwards

- "It is wiser to find out than to suppose." – Mark Twain
- "If you always put limits on everything you do, it will spread into your work and into your life. There are no limits. There are only plateaus, and you must not stay there, you must go beyond them." – Bruce Lee
- "Invest in yourself first. Expect nothing from no one and be willing to work for everything." – Tony Gaskins
- "You are responsible for your life. You can't keep blaming somebody else for your dysfunction. Life is really about moving on." – Oprah Winfrey
- "If you keep blaming something or someone else for your problems, you will never learn why problems come your way."

> **Action Steps:**
> **Identify you most common distraction that is keeping you from action and get rid of it.**

WEEK 4 – GET READY

Bold Declaration #4 - **READY:** I will make myself **READY** for challenges, knows and unknown through resources I collect.

This has been bananas delving into these depths. Do you feel what this is doing for you? It should have unearthed some of your prevalent thought patterns and called into questions may of your functional habits. You should be seeing by now how your habits have served you up until now. You should also be hungry for some new strategies on how to effectively move and drive your life forward. Doing so with the deep understanding that the condition and progress are primarily up to **YOU**. No one else and no other excuses can be acceptable.

The transformation twist to your life starts with you and the way you think about the past, present, and future. As of now, all you know is the past that has led up to the present. Some of the emotional promptings led you to this book. There is no coincidence. Nothing is random when it comes to this. You made it this far in the book because your calling needed something to sustain and guide its path. When it comes to the future, the shape of it is driven by your thoughts and actions you take. Everything you plant today will grow tomorrow. How you nurture it will determine what and how much is yielded. Your work will determine the usability.

I think it is reasonable to say, that for some of you, what you have, up until this moment has been guided by chance and hope. Based on where you were born and upbringing and access, some of you had a great start, and others of you had some major challenges. Those that have had to challenge, what I can say to you is, don't get bitter. I can sense that you want to advance. In your heart, you may feel that you need to advance and shape and awesome future for yourself and for your family legacy.

However, I head many thought leaders say that we can either feel we need something or deserve something. However, the world is tilted in favor of those that deserve. You see, there are real needs in this world. People need food, water, jobs, clothing, housings, love, friends, and peace. However, the people who end up with what they want to look at life with the deserved mentality. What that implies is that if I feel like I deserve something I have put forth the effort to support my desire. If I worked at a job, I have an agreement that clearly states that I will get an honest day's pay for an honest day's work.

In this section we are going to look at getting **READY** and addressing the question of, what do I need? This is all about being resourceful. So how does all this apply to what we deserve? Well, if you want resources to aid you in your path and navigate this transaction, then you must avoid thinking that you need something and move your attitude to that you deserve the resources you are going to get in order to move ahead. You will be encouraged to make a list of what you need and to aggressively go after what you rightfully deserve.

Imagine you are a person that has been given a call to be a runner and will be racing in a major race. Metaphorically, you are in a race for your life and future. So, you **DREAMED** of racing. Your call and alarm moved you to an **AWAKENED** state. You have an idea of what you must do. But you got to move to a state of action. So you ARISE.

Now you move on to the track. Ready to run in your big race. Like a sprinter, you move to a place and position of readiness. You make **READY** for what's about to happen. So in this segment, I am going to walk you through what it will take to get mentally ready for what's about to happen next. So, without further delay, let's get into our starting blocks…..

DAY 22 - WHAT IS IT, REALLY?

If you have been working the actions plans diligently up until this point, then you have done more than most. So, congratulation and high five, for hanging in there and making some great progress. I say that to commend you but to also warn you from here on out; it becomes more challenging. With that said....

Imaging you on a south pacific island relaxing in the tropics. Then all of a sudden you feel a shift in the atmosphere that breaks the calm and peace. The ground begins to tremble. And off in the distance, you hear a rumble. You see all around you, sighs that you are in the middle of an earthquake. You start to panic and are forced to make some urgent decisions. You go into fight or flight mode, and you skip right to the fright stage. There is no time to relax and very little margin for error. Get to safety for there is a shift in the foundation you are standing on. Action must be taken.

This is how it feels to be driven to change. You see, life is loaded with these things called transitions. We get them from the very moment we are conceived, and as a child, we're granted handlers that lead us through our transition. However, as we get older and start to make more rationalized decisions, the responsibility of how those transitions are gradually passed on to us.

Based on our training and influences, which drives how we naturally respond to life's shifts, we can either be shifted and fit into a grove, or we can choose our own destiny that serves a higher purpose and navigate the transition. One leaves us searching and wanting, and mostly, never achieving and the other, is the reason we bound out of bed every day. It feeds us for the day and fills our moments with satisfaction in how we are living our lives. We get confident that we are making a difference.

The most effective tool to use to navigate change is our minds. We are driven and moved by what we believe and what we condition our minds to respond to. We live out our beliefs by what we think. Our beliefs move us to action. Each day as we see new transitions we are challenged to question what we think we know. Many have a tendency to learn with limits and not put in the time to learn how to break past false limits or even question why the limits are there in the first place. In this day and age, we are encouraged to ask deeper, meaningful questions that show respect for the limits yet question its value and its purpose it has to play in our destiny. We get to determine if it is serving or not. We are also empowered to move limitation, simply by our beliefs.

In order to navigate the transition, we have to stay focused and keep the main thing the main thing. If we don't have the main thing, then we sure better get one. And then focus on it with all our intensity. Removing all other distraction, until we can only hear and see that of what we are focused upon and can respond to its calling. We must develop animal-like instinct and hunger when it comes to our goals. Committed to never ever give up, even in failure. Our choices define our failures and steps of faith. Ever testing the foundation upon which we stand. Moving day-by-day to higher ground. Moving from one plateau to another. Committed to success. Are your eyes fixed? Are you ready? Do you clearly know what you want? Then go out and get it!

**Positive Affirmation:
The most effective tool to use to navigate change is our minds.**

Self-Assessment Questions:

- What images come up when you think of a fixed mindset?
- What images come up when you think of a growth mindset?
- How has your core beliefs shaped your destiny and guided the path that you're on?
- If you discover that a belief no longer serves you are you free to shift it?
- If my beliefs are not what I do but what I practice, what are my practicing revealing about myself?
- What method do you use to challenge or test your beliefs?

- What techniques do you find most effective when addressing distraction and procrastination.

Branded and Bold Quotes:

- "Our greatest weakness lies in giving up. The most certain way to succeed is always to try just one more time." – Thomas A. Edison
- "The mind is a powerful force. It can enslave us or empower us. It can plunge us into the depths of misery or take us to the heights of ecstasy. Learn to use the power wisely." - David Cuscheri
- "You're mad. Bonkers. Off your head…But I'll tell you a secret…All of the best people are." – Alice In Wonderland
- "Success is not just what you accomplish in your life; it is about what you inspire others to do."
- "Don't shush your inner voice. It's who you really are."
- "Be a voice, not an echo."
- "You are what you believe yourself to be." – Paulo Coelho
- "If you ask me what I came to do in this world, I, an artist, will answer you: I am here to live out loud." – Emile Zola
- "Just when the caterpillar thought her life was over, she began to fly."
- "You don't have to be great to start, but you have to star to be great." – Zig Ziglar

> **Action Steps:**
> Get in the mirror and speak and new truth about your future. Believe in and speak it into existence.

DAY 23 - LOAD UP!

When a soldier goes into a battle, there's a lot that goes into the training as well as their mental preparedness for the mission at hand. They go through rigorous training that test and pushes past their boundaries. This is where their medal gets tested. They are faced with examining their fixed beliefs against their belief to grow. They are challenged to redefine what they know in exchange for new knowledge. At every level of training, they are pushed to set goals and focus. They realize how foundational and shaping goals are to what you do daily in order to experience said goals. They understand that the things they do today are building a block that goes into the constructing the world they will live in tomorrow.

Along with every goal that is set, there are natural obstacles and distractions that will emerge. However, along with our goals, we have to attach an emotional outcome that we want to experience in order to have what we need to address our distraction. Prior to launching into the pursuit of our goal, we have to visualize and get settled with the outcome. Not just the victory of crossing the finish line, but what is it, do we want to really feel? Why is that emotion important to us? How is this going to move or inspire those that are meaningful to our lives? Once you lock on to that emotion, that will help you see and understand your distraction, and it gives you the right thing to do with those emerging distractions.

To clearly understand we must know that change is uncomfortable to most. So when we set goals, we will subconsciously sabotage ourselves to get back into our comfort zone. So if we are not emotionally invested in our goals, we then make it easy for us to create distractions to help us deal with the pain of progress. But the distraction will come in a way that will eventually convince us to quit.

So, [text obscured] a deep seeded rec[text obscured] in every emotion th[text obscured] need to call that e[text obscured] do and every element that we can. Once you lock your mind on something, you then have the ultimate tool, power, and weapon to accomplish anything. There is nothing like the power of a changed mind.

Positive Affirmation:
If you want to hit your goals easier, you must emotionally invest in them.

Self-Assessment Questions:

- What have natural life situations played a part in conditioning me?
- These events in my life have conditioned me to think like a champion....?

- What are some events that have pushed you past your limits? What did you learn about yourself?
- Do you practice more of a fixed or a growth belief mindset?
- What are courageous steps of habits you taking daily?
- What emotion do you expect to feel once you reached your top goal?

Branded and Bold Quotes:

- "Strength does not come from winning. Your struggles develop your strengths. When you go through hardships and decide not to surrender, that is true strength." – Arnold Schwarzenegger
- "The quickest way to acquire self-confidence is to do exactly what you are afraid to do."
- "A winner is someone who recognizes his God-given talents, works his tail off to develop them into skills and uses these skills to accomplish his goals." – Larry Bird
- "The comeback is always stronger than the setback."
- "When you love what you have, you have everything you need."
- "It took me quite a long time to develop a voice, and now that I have it, I am not going to be silent." – Madeline Albright
- "Successful people are not gifted; they just work hard, then succeed on purpose."

> "Sometimes, you need to step outside, get some are, and remind yourself of who you are and who you want to be."
> "Discipline is just choosing between what you want, now and what you want most."
> "If you haven't found it yet, keep looking." – Steve Jobs

Action Steps:
Go ask a close personal friend and ask if the think if you seem distracted.

DAY 24 - CHOOSE THE CHALLENGE

Change is necessary! To manage your life brand, you must come to terms that to get what you want, which you may not have today is a change but with every change comes challenge. There is no way your brain is going to let you disrupt the comfort that it has known just of you to have something that is so unfamiliar and unknown. Therefore, you will be torn between that which you want and the life your brain wants you to maintain. And like a good soldier, you got to get real about war.

War will claim lives and hurt the innocent. But an enemy is only as powerful as we chose to let it be. So today, make a declaration to stand up against tourney. You see, we feel threatened to do something different outside of our norm. But, if we know that there is more and we stay the same, then our very soul will die. For as you see, there is a fate worse than death. For when we find ourselves still living, but watching portions of ourselves die day-by-day, simply because we choose not to move or get up and live life, that is state of being a living dead.

Change is the medicine. If you find that your life is dull, boring, or, if you feel like you are fading or mediocre, then it is time for a change challenge. Just like any of the other challenges that exist in the world to promote awareness or to transform a life, you are being challenged to take today and really go to work on your personal transformation. Instead of running from it, turn around and press in.

Become relentless. Identify what you want and come to terms with why you need to change so badly. Focus and go to work on you. Put so much work in on yourself that if you were to look in the mirror in the next 30 days, you would not be able to recognize you. Change does not have to take long. You could make significant changes in 30 days. An effective way to make a 30-day change is the pick someone you would like to model and practice at least one of their habits for 30 days. You would be blown away by how much you can change within that time frame, but if you did a different 30-day challenge in a year, how much different would your life be by that time. At the end of each challenge, examine the results. See if it lines up with your WHY. If it does then, it should be easier to keep the habit. So, plot the course, step up and make your move. Don't fear change owning you. Face the challenge and go and claim your prize.

Positive Affirmation:
Living while hoping and never acting upon our desire is fate worse than death.

Self-Assessment Questions:

- I feel it is more important that I change than my circumstances because....?
- I feel it is more important that my circumstances change than myself because.....?
- I have a strong passion and desire to have to do the following....?
- How willing have I been in the past to change in order to get what I wanted?
- In previous attempt to change a habit or move forward, what were the things that distracted you or set you back?
- What comes to mind when you think if going to war with yourself?
- It what way does it bother you when you have not worked on or achieved your desired change?
- When making changes, what has helped you the most, willpower, brute force, or increased intelligence?
- If you put forth your best strategies, what life changes could you make over the next 30 days?

Branded and Bold Quotes:

> "I always wonder why birds choose to stay in the same place when they can fly anywhere on the earth. Then I ask myself the same questions." – Harun Yahya

- "Life is either a daring adventure or nothing at all."
- "Behind you are the challenges you've met. Before you lies new possibilities. Today you choose the direction of your life."
- "Look at a day when you are supremely satisfied at the end. It's not a day when you lounge around doing nothing; it's a day you've had everything to do, and you've done it."
- "A challenge becomes an obstacle when you bow to it."
- "The man on the top of the mountain didn't fall there." – Vince Lombardi
- "If it doesn't challenge you, it won't change you."
- "Don't pray for an easy life. Pray for the strength to endure a difficult one." – Bruce Lee
- "Your power to choose your direction of your life allows you to reinvent yourself, to change your future, and to powerfully influence the rest of creation." – Stephen Covey
- "Running away from any problem only increases the distance from the solution. The easiest way to escape from the problem is to solve it."

Action Steps:
Practice a new habit that matches your WHY for the next 30 days.

DAY 25 - LIMITING LIMITS

What are limits and why is it important to understand what they mean to our existence? .First of all, limits are there to serve us. The common misconceptions are that limits are a negative thing. However, limits, when used, are there to function as guides, indicators and even safety to real dangers. Yet, if we are going to have limits in our lives all must be tested, mastered and assigned.

Limits live inside of a story. We humans communicate, thrive and drive based on a series of stories. A story moves all that we have see and do. The story of when, where and how we will stop in life is directly associated with how it's told and how limits fit within a given story.

Limits are like a strong-willed and vicious dog that imposes fear but when placed in the hands of a person who knows dogs, can be managed and harnessed in a way that the noise and power they possess is focused toward a more meaningful purpose. A muzzled dog becomes instantaneously harmless. Imagine that for a moment. The fear of that animal is instantaneously removed once the muzzle has been put in place. That's what you need to do with your limits. Muzzle the stories. Better yet, change your role in the story. Instead of being the victim, become the handler.

You need to watch your head language. If you are dealing with absolutes, then you are willfully moving in the realm of limits. Always and never, are words that are associated with things you will always or never accomplish. Those words are hollow as the ones that said that man would NEVER walk on the moon. It took a story and belief to change that.

Focus! This is vital to moving past your limits. You have to clearly know your goals. But you also have to link your goals to a WHY that moves you emotionally. But if you want to give your focus a bit more kick, give it to someone. What I mean by that is in this example. Let's say you wanted to run a marathon on behalf of someone who has no legs but they have a desire to run. That would give you connection and a drive and determination to never quit. It goes beyond you, your stories and beliefs. So, find a cause that is so compelling to link it to, and you will never give up.

Visualize hard. Make your future outcome so real, that you can touch. Smell, hear, taste and fully experience it. If you can deeply visualize the success, your mind will come up with a way to make it possible.

Get that Edge! How is strength develop? When you have lifted to the point of breakdown, and you discover that there is nothing left. Then you dig into your goals and reach down inside yourself, and you call out for one more. Just one more. That's the edge. You put your discipline at this level, committed to fighting for a new edge every day; then you will become an unlimited, unstoppable force.

Now that you have the clue to get the new story, you also are realizing that you are now free from the prison of your own mind. You are free to become or do anything you literally can set your mind to. All it takes is a good story attached to the right motives and an intelligent strategy. Limits! Bye-bye. Time to step into your destiny.

> **Positive Affirmation:**
> **Limits only live inside a temporary story**

Self-Assessment Questions:

- What are some limitations you have struggled with?
- Are your limitations tangible objects or mentally imposed?
- In your attempt to surpass the limits, what have you learned about your ability?
- How have you used limits to your advantage?
- Along with your limits, what story have you grown accustomed to telling about it?
- How detailed are you with your limitation story?
- How often have you told that limitation story this past week/
- What's a better roll you could play within a limiting story?
- Do you find yourself placing absolutes upon your limits?
- WHO are the WHY's in your life?
- How tangible have you made your vision?

- In what areas of your life are you being challenged to dig deeper than you have ever gone before?
- What new and empowering story are you ready to tell yourself?

Branded and Bold Quotes:

- "You are your only limit."
- "The pain you feel today will be the strength you feel tomorrow."
- "Yesterday you said tomorrow."
- "Impossible only means that you haven't found the solution yet." – Anonymous
- "You are only confined b the walls you build yourself."
- "Failure is not the opposite of success. It's part of success."
- "Success always comes when preparation meets opportunity." – Henry Hartman
- "If it wasn't hard, everyone would do it. It's the hard that makes it great."
- "Never limit yourself because of others limited imagination; Never limit others because of your own limited imagination." – Mae Jemison
- "Never put an age limit on your dreams."

Action Steps:
List the people that motivate you and are the reason that you keep going.

DAY 26 - TRANSFORM FROM THE INSIDE OUT

Change is a natural part of living. We are encouraged to change from the outside or inside. From birth till now we have been going through changes. At the physical level, we had natural occurrences and much of what we did, we found ourselves compelled to do, such as eat or take our very first step. As we got older and had to take an active role in our destiny, we found it to be challenging because we were walking into the unknown. Fear united with the unknown can halt our natural progress. It's in our DNA to grow and transform. When we allow ourselves to settle we also can introduce anxiety into our lives rooted in longing but never doing.

We all are blessed with the means to transform, grow and evolve. We were born with a will and an ability to focus. Where the mind goes energy flows. That energy transforms us. We can put on an exterior act, but anything that exists on the outside is always driven by the internal. Therefore we need to get solid and steadfast in what we want and who we what to be and how we need to change in order to achieve. Each day, we must turn up the fire in our hearth. Heat our medal and lay it on the anvil of our life and hammer away at it till we are forged, shaped and transformed into our calling. Let the fire and pressure refine us into our personal calling.

If not challenged our minds can function as a prison. We get sentenced and locked in a mode or cell, conditioning us to live a confined life. Our limiting thoughts become our prison. Knowledge liberates and pardons us. Hope opens the cell doors and tells us to go free. But until you choose that you are free and authorized to excel, true freedom cannot be achieved. So, understand that by the power of your minds dwelling are you transformed.

What is your identity selection? What label do you give yourself? What is your designation in the world you live in? In fact, do you call how you are living your life, really living? In a play or movie you will have many roles but vitally key parts. You have victims, monsters, hero, guides, or sage. Each role has its significant place. If your life was a stage play, what role would you play? Oh, I forgot, there's the director as well. If you were directing your own life, how would you reassign your role? It doesn't take a lot of time; it just takes a choice and some action. So, move and change, today!

Positive Affirmation:
If not challenged our minds can function as a prison.

Self-Assessment Questions:

- In what ways have you changed over the past 10 years?
- In what ways have you changed over the past 1 years?
- In what ways have you changed in the past year?
- How dramatic was the change in what you believed then to what you believe now?
- Have you gotten stronger in your beliefs or do you find yourself struggling even more?
- In what areas of your life to do FEAR change and how is that associated to what you may lose?
- If you were to assign your current role in life a general title, what would be the name of that role?
- If you were to assign your expected future role in life a general title, what would be the name of that role?

Branded and Bold Quotes:

- "If an egg is broken by an outside force, life ends. If broken by an inside force, life begins. Great things always begin from the inside."
- "Don't wait around for other people to be happy for you. Any happiness you get you've got to make yourself." – Alice Walker
- "To reach a great height a person needs to have great depth."
- "I begin with an idea, and then it becomes something else." – Pablo Picasso
- "Creativity is thinking up new things. Innovation is doing new things."

- "Don't compare yourself to others. Compare to yourself to the person from yesterday."
- "Take it slow and give your soul a chance to catch up with your body."
- "The hardest battle you will ever have to fight is between who you are now and who you want to be."
- "No great thing is suddenly created." – Epictetus
- "If nothing ever changed, there'd be no butterflies." – Unknown

---

**Action Steps:
Make a list of limiting words and statements you have used in the past and commit to NEVER use them again.**

DAY 27 - GREATER GROWTH

To be honest, growth is not an easy thing. As a child's body grows, they experience actual growing pains, where the rate of their growth exceeds the rate of the nerve growth and it causes pain. There is also pain associated with the growth in knowledge. Some struggle with learning new concepts and it produces anxieties. As adults, we are faced with choices, and many of the choices require us to take risk. The risk we take, whether we fail or succeed, produces growth.

This journey you are on, for some, it is a call to go against the grain of what you were taught or even what you believe down to your core. In order to pursue some of these exercises, you will be called up to perform an act of courage. And exercise of action that moves you out of your comfort zone and into the fire, it seems at times. The fire of refinement that is used to mold a shape our identity as well as our destiny. It takes a brave person to do what I am asking you to do.

You may be called to start a business. You may be moved to start an exercise program that could save your life. You may be called to sit down with your spouse and tell them how you struggle with how you feel about them. You may be called to have a heart-to-heart with your parents and tell them that you want to pursue a college major that is not what they had picked out. You may be called to step away from the family business. You may be called to confront your boss and insist on better working conditions or even better pay for the value you bring.

Growth, change, and courage goes hand-in-hand. You need to find your strength and your voice. You are being called to action. This is where it gets difficult. You see, most will get the call, but within a matter of seconds, they talk themselves out of it. You have to stop the chatter. Today is the day you listen to the voice of your destiny and take the leap. Take action on your future. Time to stop settling.

If your future and best you were to hop in a time machine and come back to you right now, what would the tell you to do? What would they tell you to say? The action you take right now is a direct indicator of how fast and how strong you will grow. Remove all barriers and kill the excuses. Today is your day. Go grow. Go take action. Roar like a lion and display your courage. Reach into the future and grasp what was meant for you to have.

Positive Affirmation:
The action you take right now is a direct indicator of how fast and how strong you will grow.

Self-Assessment Questions:

- In order for you to reach your goals, what will you have to risk in order to get there?
- Are you OK with taking risk?
- How do you determine if a risk is worth it before you take action?
- You goals pull you out of your comfort zone. What are the things that lay out there that are of concern to you?
- Do you feel you are being called to a place that is outside of your family or social norms? How does that make you feel? Is it worth it to take the adventure?
- What would your future self-have of you to do?

Branded and Bold Quotes:

- "What other people think of you is not your business. If you start to make that business your business, you will be offended for the rest of your life." – Deepak Chopra
- "Rock bottom became the solid foundation on which I rebuilt my life." – J.K. Rowling
- "The only person you are destined to become is the person you decide to be." – Ralph Waldo Emmerson
- "The difficulty lies not so much in developing new ideas as in escaping from old ones." – John Maynard Keynes
- "The most successful people learn something new each day. Knowledge is endless, and

personal growth is continuous. Always seek more." – Brooke Griffin
- "The smallest of actions is always better than the noblest of intentions." – Robin Sharma
- "You must take personal responsibility. You cannot change the circumstances, the seasons, or the wind, but you can change yourself that is something you have charge of." – Jim Rohn
- "How wonderful it is that nobody need wait a single moment to improve the world." – Anne Frank
- "To accomplish great things, we must not only act but also dream: not only plan but also believe." – Anatole France
- "The best way to capture moments is to pay attention. This is how we cultivate mindfulness. Mindfulness means being awake. It means knowing what you are doing" – Jon Kabat-Zinn
- There are no failures – Just experiences and your reactions to them." – Tom Krause

> **Action Steps:**
> **Seek council from your future self.**
> **Whatever they say, don't hesitate.**
> **Do it!!**

DAY 28 - IF YOU NEED IT…

Taking charge and leadership of your destiny is not easy task. All you know is what is behind you, and for the most part, you have heard stories and seen firsthand, tales of failures. The possibilities are limited because you haven't practiced venturing into the unknown. We are conditioned to stay within the lines and function with parameters that are clear and obvious and others that are perceived. We are trained to see scarcities.

However, as we move into the realm of marketing and establishing our brand, we have to do it boldly and with declaration. We have to declare and believe internally in what we are doing and why we are doing it. We have to develop a sense of focus, that is unwavering. We then have to move into an area of maturating where we go on the attack of our limitation.

When we start to use the word "TOO" in description of when something is going a certain way, or not, getting done, we need to realize we are only looking at our resources. Our age, race, height, gender, weight, money, time, education, tools, so forth and so on, are things that we claim we are lacking so we use these as excuses for not reaching our goals. What we choose to DO with our resources is where we become resourceful. We strip of the limits and get down and dirty and figure out what we can do with what we have.

If you want to enhance your resourcefulness, hang around resourceful people. Read stories of what others have done. Look at creative ways they have solved their problem. As often as you can, read and study other great problem solvers. This will push your creative juices so you can come up with what you need to solve problems.

A person who is resourceful regularly practices dreaming. They go deep into their imagination, and they don't take any vision for granted. They write every idea down. Even if they don't act on it, they at least get it out of there head and place it on paper. And as they plot through life, they then can recall one of those bright ideas to see where it can fit and be of usefulness in any given situation. They hone their mind for the right opportunity.

A person who is resourceful spends a lot of time building networks. Examining the skills and refocuses within a given network. So, as the task arises, they have at their fingertips, resources they can align to get in front of any given problem. Resourcefulness is not making due with less; it is mainly managing what you have effectively.

Positive Affirmation:
If you want to enhance your resourcefulness, hang around resourceful people.

Self-Assessment Questions:

- Have you recognized your call to lead?
- I have had experience with leading in the following areas….?
- In my calling it will require me to lead in the following areas…..?
- I am aware that I have been conditioned to function within these certain parameters….?
- Those parameters have served me in the following areas….?
- Those parameters have limited me from experiencing….?
- In what ways have you marketed who you are and the areas where you were designed to serve?
- What resources do you have at your disposal?
- What method of thinking do you use when seeking out new resources?
- How important is it to you to seek out resources?
- These are the people I admire in how the exercise their level of resourcefulness….?
- How has networking been of value to you in the past?

Branded and Bold Quotes:

> "Change the changeable, accept the unchangeable, and remove yourself from the unacceptable."

- "If you don't leave your past in the past, it will destroy your future. Live for what today has to offer not for what yesterday has taken away."
- "The struggle you're in today is developing the strength you need for tomorrow."
- "Look closely at the present you are constructing. It should look like the future you are dreaming." – Alice Walker
- "In school, we learn first before we take the test. In life, we take the test first before we learn."
- "Education is the most powerful weapon which you can use to change the world." – Nelson Mandela
- "Anyone who stops learning is old, whether at twenty or eighty. Anyone who keeps learning stays young." – Henry Ford
- "Dreams are lovely, but they are just dreams. Fleeting, ephemeral, pretty. But dreams do not come true just because you dream them it's hard work that makes things happen. It's hard work that creates change."
- "Just believe in yourself. Even if you don't pretend that you do and at some point, you will." – Venus Williams
- "You have within you, right now, everything you need to deal with whatever the world can throw at you."

Action Steps:
Find 5 highly motivated resourceful people and schedule a meeting with them this week and discuss methods they use to network with others.

WEEK 5 – GET SET

Bold Declaration #5 - **SET:** I will **SET** my focus, plan, and commitment and will only settle for success.

Well, you have been crushing it so far. Do you feel it? There should be a level of excitement. The questions that you have been addressing should have revealed some deeply seated truths. Some of the questions should have revealed to you how empowered you are. Some of your circumstances may be challenging, but you have a spirit and a drive that can burst through any of the challenges.

I am excited for each of you. You are moving to a place of some real action. We can sit and think and plan our future. We can become so good at the planning part that we create frustration through discouragement. But until we get out of our seats and the move into position, we will never fully experience what it means to feel alive and satisfied. We've come too far to stop now. We are too close to the finish.

We must be compelled to move to action as fast as possible and as often as possible. This is foundational to changing our world. It is the hallmark of your brand. You will be measured more by what you do than what you say you will do. If you find yourself saying what you will do more than taking action, that will reflect upon your brand as well. It will label you as either lazy, complacent, lacking direction or passion, but overall, it will not serve any value.

Work must be the order of the day. In this section, we are talking about moving into the starting blocks and getting into position to execute. Getting SET! That is we are doing. Getting laser-like focus. We ask where is our focus? We have hinted on much of what we will talk about in this section in the previous section, but here is where we get focused. Before you can effectively execute, there are a few things to consider.

We will get solid on being determined. Knowing that there will be temptations in your race to either pursuance you to not be in the race or that you are not worthy to be on the field. You will hear that there is no way for you do what you are hoping to accomplish. You will hear that the competition is too fierce among a plethora of other determinants. Here is where you put on the fighters game face.

You get mad-dog fierce and you, without blinking, get into the face of your opponent. You go dark and dead in your own eyes. You show your opposition their future. This is where you become resilient and rock solid in your commitment to deliver. Once the bell rings, there is no other option but to win, no matter what it cost you or how bad it will hurt. You will get hit and maybe even knocked down, but commit today that you will not quit. Commit to showing up for every round. Holding nothing back.

You have trained for this event. You have put in the miles. You have lifted the weight. You have hit the bag. You have spared. Today is fight day. Will you get in the ring and bring it!?!? DING DING! Time to go to work……

DAY 29 - WHERE IS YOUR FOCUS?

"Focus" is a common word but with it comes to managing life, we can tend to find it difficult to execute. As you see, we are wired for survival and comfort. To manage your life brand means that you are moving from where you are to where you want to be. In order to get there, you have to focus on your objective. That term has been around for a very long time. But the very moment we choose to make a change, we must understand that any and all change comes with distractions. Distractions that will enable our subconscious to recognize that will enable us to get back into our comfort zone. So in order to have what it takes to hit what you're focused upon, some elements have to attach to that focus.

We first must attach clarity. The thing that we want to achieve, we must know it in detail. We have to get to the point where when we close our eyes we can see, smell, and taste and embrace that which we desire. Focus and desire go hand in hand. It just that desire moves us to re realm of obsession. Once we become obsessed with something, we lock on and cannot let it go, until the thirst has been quenched.

Next, we must attach a WHY to that which we want. We have to have motives for pursuit. What does it matter at all if we hit our mark?

With that WHY, we also need to set a WHO. These are the people that it matters to if we hit our mark or note. How are we going to impact their lives? If we fail, in what way will we let them down? We have to have a reason bigger than ourselves, to keep us going as we press ahead.

Next, once you get your objective fixed, you then have to devise a detailed plan on how you will get there.

Obsession should be a word that you marry to focus. For to have the kind of drive you need to succeed in this distracted environment, you will need to become fixed and obsession with the thing that you want. Bear in mind that the obsession should only last for a season. Once you get there, assess where you are, who you are and evaluate the importance of that goal to your new identity? Use that obsession as fuel.

You will be tempted to multitask, but it has been proven that there is no such thing as multitasking, even with computers. All multitasking is meant is to work faster and harder at splitting the difference. However, that waters down the human's ability to hit their objective effectively, and it introduces distractions that could have you hitting the wrong target.

You will hear leaders say, keep the main thing, the main thing. To some, the goal is the main thing, but to the true-life brand manager, you will find that it is your identity transformation to be the main thing.

Who will you become?

> **Positive Affirmation:**
> **F.O.C.U.S. – Follow One Couse Until Successful**

Self-Assessment Questions:

- When you focus on a task, what aids you in maintaining your focus?
- If you knew and anticipated that you were going to get distracted how could that aid you with remaining focused?
- How can strong emotional pain and pleasure be of value to you with maintaining focus?
- When you set your goals to a date and measure our progress, you get better results. How has setting dated goals help you in the past?
- Check your daily progress: Does your activity relate to you stated and focused goals?
- Feelings are deceiving – Feelings will lead to comfort. How do you think this could put you at risk when pressing toward your goals?
- Do you regularly focus on objectives or limits?
- Do you focus on your progress or more on your failures?
- Do you focus on what you need to do or do you focus on who you need to be in order to do what you MUST do?

✎ Do you focus on your dreams or your fears?

Branded and Bold Quotes:

- "When you focus on problems, you'll have more problems. When you focus on possibilities, you'll have more opportunities."
- "The real voyage of discovery consists not in seeking new lands, but seeking with new eyes."
- "The future belongs to those who believe in the beauty of their dreams."
- "The greatest danger for most of us is not that our aim is too high and we miss it but that it is too low and we reach it." – Michelangelo
- "Sometimes you have to lose y our mind in order to find your freedom."
- "All you need in this life is ignorance and confidence, and then success is sure." – Mark Twain
- "Don't downgrade your dream to match your reality, upgrade your faith to match your destiny."
- "It's a terrible thing, I think, in life to wait until you're ready. I have this feeling now that actually no one is ever ready to do anything. There is almost no such thing as ready. There is only now.
- "It is the set of the sails, not the direction of the wind that determines which way we will go. – Jim Rohn
- "One way to keep momentum going is to have constantly greater goals." – Michael Korda

Action Steps:
List out in detail that which you want to achieve. Next, make a vision board and look at it every day.

DAY 30 - CHUNK IT!

Mount Everest! It has been climbed by many and has claimed the lives of many. It is a mountain to be respected. It is no easy task to ascend this great wonder of the world. It takes months of training and physical conditioning to scale this massive hill. It requires guides and resources. It's no joke. When looking at it from the base, it looks overwhelming and feels near impossible to climb. Yes, as climbers have ascended this great mountain, they discover that there are paths, and trails made by others who have gone before, as well as there, are opening and crevasses used as footings to leverage yourself up.

Bit by bit, step-by-step. Each step gives hope and reassurance of the possibility of reaching the summit. It takes several days to go from base to summit. A guide will have the climbers cover so many yards per day. Nothing more and nothing less. Rest breaks are allocated in order to let the climbers reset. A high amount of calories are consumed in order to replenish what was used during the assent.

This gives us a clue as to the power of chunking. Chunking is where you take a massive goal and break it down into manageable, bite-size chunks. Each chunk gives a timeline. This technique is not new. It has been around for many years, but as of lately, there has been a closer association with the effectiveness and productivity.

When we break things down and attack them, it produces this psychological effect that sparks encouragement and a level of accomplishment. It keeps you in the habit of motion, but not overwhelming you through the process. Along the task path, there are breaks that should be scheduled in order to give the plan balance.

When the chunks are broken down, it is a great strategy to plane as much critical stuff early in your day. That way, if there is slippage, it won't generate too much stress, and you have means to catch it before the day gets away from you.

As you start to engage with your chunks, it is crucial to identify you potential distractions and roadblocks. If managed early, you can dispatch your distractions before they even get a chance to get o started.

Chunking is simplistic but extremely powerful. Especially in the area of project/resource management. As you work on your chunk with passion and not concentrate on the mountain too much, but pay attention to your footings, you will be in a position to accomplish your overall task ahead of schedule.

> **Positive Affirmation:**
> **Fall in love with the process and the results will come.**

Self-Assessment Questions:

- What big goals have you set lately? Are they big enough or can you make them bigger?
- How descriptive can you be with the details of your goals?
- Each element of the detail can be broken down into smaller chunks. So how many chunks can you make out of your detail?
- Do you practice delaying tough or challenging work?
- Do you have any fears associated with failure as your reason for the delay?
- What results do you think you could get if you placed the critical work at the top of your priority list?
- When you broke the thing down in the past what emotional benefit did you get from taking it that way?

Branded and Bold Quotes:

- "Ideas are like rabbits. You get a couple and learn how to handle them, and pretty soon you have a dozen." – John Schinbeck
- "Fall in love with the process and the results will come."
- "You may not realize it, but by chasing your goals and never giving up, you're inspiring others to do the same."
- "You're off to great places. Today is your day. Your mountain is waiting, so get on your way." – Dr. Seuss
- "If you want to be truly successful invest in yourself to get the knowledge you need to find your unique factor. When you find it and focus on it and persevere your success will blossom." – Sydney Madwed
- "Be patient with yourself. Self-growth is tender; it's holy ground. There's no greater investment…" – Stephen Covey
- "A year from now you will wish you had started today."
- "Success is the sum of small efforts, repeated day-in & day-out."
- "Successful people are not gifted; they just work hard, then succeed on purpose."
- "Timing, perseverance, and ten years of trying will eventually make you look like an overnight success." Biz Stone

---

Action Steps:
Take your toughest project and break it down into 5 to 10 mini goals. Set those to a date.

DAY 31 - OVERCOME OBSTACLES

You find yourself waking up, alone in a dark room. A sense of fear and frustration comes over you. Why are you here? There is no good reason for you to be in this place. You call out. "Is any here?" No reply. Because of the echo, you know that you are in a room. You shuffle over to the nearest wall in the dimly lit location. You feel that it's made of cinder blocks. You feel along the wall to see if there's a door. Oddly enough, there is no door. You realize that you are in a sealed room. What kind if torcher is this? You ask.

With the fear came the response. You could either get frightened and shut down, or you can run and hide, but there is no place to hide, or you can fight. However, there is no one in the room with you that you need to fight. All that you know is that you are boxed in for no good reason, and the natural instinct is to get out. But how? There are no tools so what can you do. The best response is to stop and think. Size up the objective, opposition, and options.

The room is a metaphor for how we feel trapped at times in situations. When we are trapped, we go into story mode. Most have conditioned themselves to go into worst case story. We look for how bad we are stuck instead of looking at the various options to freedom. Before we move, we need to clearly define what it is that we really want to do. We need to define a win. If the win is not obvious, then we need to reset the parameters. We need to reframe the solution to make the win manageable. We need to know what we want and what is at stake. Overall, we need to establish a vision and reason to pursue that vision.

When we have an objective, which in this case, we want to be free of the room in which we have been held captive against our will. In this case, it is easy to get caught up on casting blame as to why you are in a situation, but that is limiting, and it is disempowering. It easy to say, "Why is this happening to me?" However, that statement lacks maturity, and it places way too much power in the hands of events as well as other people. Some could respond and say "This is happening for me." As if this is an event that is trying to teach me a lesson. However, events are just sometimes events. We then may conclude a lesson when the class is not in session.

A much stronger reproach is to say "This event is happening because of me." Take change and ownership of all situations you are in. This is a bold move and an act of responsibility. It may be true that someone may have done something to you with intent to harm you. However, if you take ownership of what is happening to you, then it puts you in the position of power. You gain power over events, circumstances, and others. It allows you to manage events better. It moves you to a place of allowing your ultimate problem-solving machine to go to work.

This is where options come in. You can then freely think of a way to solve your own problem since you were the one who created your problem. You can develop the mind to seek out newer and better solutions. So instead of saying you are trapped in a room, you could say, "how did I place myself in this room?" "Is there a door hidden somewhere in a nonconventional spot?" , "Since I have no tools, what part of my body could I used to make a door?" When free to think then the options become unlimited.

Obstacles are only stories that simply have not been challenged with a happy ending.

> **Positive Affirmation:**
> **Obstacles have no choice but to give way to determination.**

Self-Assessment Questions:

- Why are you giving your obstacle a name? (At this point it should be dead to you)
- What plans have you made to destroy what's in your way?
- Are your goals worth pursuing in comparison to the obstacles that are trying to stop you?
- What are you willing to sacrifice in order to experience a breakthrough?
- How did you silence those that told you to give up or give in to an obstacle?

- Do you have a belief that can see through walls?
- What can your mind do with the belief that everything that happens is done because of you?
- What story of victory are you rehearsing in your mind at this moment? Is there a way to make it louder?
- List your external resources that you can call on to aid you in going through, removing or destroying your obstacle?
- When stuck you may need to get out of your own head. So, who else's response can you call upon to mentally guide you, by their example of problem-solving?
- If you want to feel like a winner, then count your previous wins. What do you have to be grateful for and things have you done, where you have experienced success?
- Do you spike the ball when you score touchdowns in your life? Do you celebrate every little win?
- Do you subscribe to distractions and procrastination? How has that aided you temporary and long-term?

Branded and Bold Quotes:

- "One of the quickest ways to acquire self-confidence is to do exactly what you are afraid to do."
- "I'm stronger because I had to be, I'm smarter because of my mistakes, happier because of the

sadness I've known, and now wiser because I learned"
- "The struggle of life is one of the greatest blessings. It makes us patient, sensitive, and Godlike. It teaches us that although the world is full of suffering, it is also full of the overcoming of it." – Hellen Keller
- "Life will beat you up a lot so be proud of each and every trial you came through. The physical and emotional scars of those trials are medals of bravery for not giving up."
- "Obstacles do not block the path; they are the path."
- "Acceptance of what has happened is the first step to overcoming the consequences of any misfortune." – William James
- "The biggest obstacle you'll ever have to overcome is your mind. If you can overcome that, you can overcome anything."
- "Our greatest glory is not in never falling, but in rising every time, we fall." – Confucius
- Challenges are what make life interesting. Overcoming them is what makes them meaningful."
- "Strength doesn't come from what you can do. It comes from overcoming the things you once thought you couldn't." – Rikki Rogers
- "Nobody can judge effort. Effort is between you and you."

Action Steps:
Declare that most of your obstacles are internal and go to war with them. Make a battle plan and execute it!

DAY 32 - REFUSE TO BOW

Life has been a little intense for you lately. You feel as if your efforts have gone unappreciated. There are days when you have opened your mouth ready to present a great idea that could help your team, but the words would not come out, or it felt as if no one was listening to you. You've been hearing voices in your head, not of today, but of your past, saying, "You're not good enough.", "Why are you so slow?", "We don't need your kind around here...", "You're worthless and need to go somewhere and die...".

The voice from yesterday seems to haunt you like a ghost from Charles Dickens, Christmas Carole. But instead of bringing hope they bring demise. You want to bow and give in. Part of you wants to get angry and fight back. But what good would that do? Make you aggressive as the people and leaders that have tried to break and oppress you? Some, who were well-meaning, wounded you deeply in your spirit. They were loud and overbearing. But who chose to give their tone or words meaning? You did! Did you forget that you have been granted a higher and nobler calling? What about those people and customers you were granted the highest responsibility to serve? Will you let an aggressive person who is so temporary and weak in communication steal from you and take from those that you support? NO! No, you will not.

Today, you were granted a newer and higher calling. You seek the WIN-WIN-WIN in everything you do. You are not going to be selfish and seek a win for yourself. Because if you do, you will only be aggressive or manipulative as others have been to you. You are not going to cower and bow down and seek the win just for the other person and further inflate their ego. In order for evil to win all it takes is for a good man to do nothing. Your passion is for the trifecta. You seek a win for yourself, a win for the other person and you push for the higher call which is the win for how what you are going to do will impact the lives of others.

You see, when you chose to valiantly serve humanity, and progressively seek effective ways to deliver service, it's as if you were taking the people you serving, who have a need, and place them on your shoulders. Making a path to success, people and obstacles miraculously get out of your way. For, you cannot stop a person with a purpose that is higher than themselves. Serving others is your leverage to success.

Assertiveness will be your key. However, assertiveness is not wining to get your way. Assertive is mastery of communication of objectives and needs. If you can clearly state at every lever the needs of your customer and show that you are passionate about meeting their needs as well as what is required to serve that needs. Those that want to tower over you will be silenced by your desire to lead and serve. So, to serve with passion is not bowing down or giving up, but it is really rising up to a new level of maturity in that it fully recognizes why we're all here to serve one another.

A passion to serve transcends gender, culture, race, age, ethnicity and financial status. It breaks down barriers and if communicated effectively, becomes contagious. When a person serves their fellow man, it moves and inspires others. So how will you assert yourself today? How will you serve?

> **Positive Affirmation:**
> **Aggressive behavior bows to assertive service.**

Self-Assessment Questions:

- What if that aggressive person is y our boss or customer?
- If you choose to be submissive, how does that serve the immediate and the long-term situation?
- Do you have reactions that serve or undermine your ego or does your ego support or undermine your reactions?
- Opinion: How important is it to express yourself from your ego?
- What modification to your skills do you need to make to manage the influx of egotistical expressions of others?

- When making decisions, do you base the foundation on your planned goals or do you do it primarily for tribal compliance?
- How do you use your assertiveness in order to achieve balance?
- When you choose to stand up for yourself do you ever feel that it is a representation of others who wish they could stand?'
- Examine your common expressions: Do you sense that the tone makes you come off like a victim, monster or victorious?
- How has being passive improved communication? What real value does it bring to any given situation?
- Do you say NO in order to promote balance and quality of what you bring to the world?
- If aggression is used to make others shrink, what should be done to manage those that practice it?
- If aggressive expression indicates that a person is in need of communication assistance, how can you better aid them in what they are trying to express?

Branded and Bold Quotes:

> "Champions don't show up to get everything they want; they show up to give everything they have."
> "Someday you will look back and know exactly why it had to happen."
> "You can never progress if you are letting things that don't deserve your attention continue to bring you down."

- "Every mountain top is within reach if you just keep climbing." – Barry Finlay
- "Without the rain, there would be no rainbow." – Gilbert Chesterton
- "You must find the place inside yourself where nothing is impossible." – Deepak Chopra
- "It's hard to beat a person who never gives up." – Babe Ruth
- "It is going to be hard but hard is not impossible."
- "Success in life comes when you simply refuse to give up, with goals so strong that obstacles, failure, and loss only act as motivation.
- "In order to be successful, your focus has to be so intense; people think you're crazy."

Action Steps:
Listen for aggressive expression in yourself and others and creatively come up with a better way to communicate.

DAY 33 - FIGHT THE ENEMY WITHIN

What people see you do is a minor reflection of what's going on inside. When you perform an act of kindness without being promoted is a direct reflection of the magnitude of the joy and gratitude in your heart. In contrast, if you were to emotionally snap on a friend or coworker for no good reason also indicates the level of rage and chaos that is stirring in your soul. Your physical expression is a window into your soul.

There is a term that is tossed around and used quite loosely. The term is "Being transparent." I have seen people use it as a means to pour out one's soul to another exposing all their deep dark secrets. However, I have seen it miss used in such that one person would tell another person to be more transparent so they can hear a deep dark secret that they can exploit and manipulate.

True transparency begins within. This is where you commit to never lie to yourself. You examine every story you think, along with others you tell, demanding the highest level of honesty, not for other's sake, but for your own. Once a person chooses to be honest, they are then positioned for ownership and empowerment.

To internally demand honesty promotes outward honesty. It exposes strengths and weaknesses. It reveals what must be worked on. It shows vulnerability, but it doesn't promote your weaknesses for manipulation. This revelation is an opportunity for applied courage. It takes courage, to be honest. It takes courage to decide to see a problem. It takes courage to take action on your problem. Real transparency promotes a courageous lifestyle. A life of action toward a positive development. It takes courage to go to war against your own noted flaws. When you valiantly go to war with yourself, you create a spectacle. Something noteworthy. An event that others will stop and watch. You see, people can respect those that get real about working on one's self.

Vulnerability means we choose to get real and not fake it till we make it or deny certain feelings and emotion, but instead, we choose to jump in and examine the value of every emotion. By processing all emotions, good and painful, we produce a more refined product that can withstand practically anything the world can throw at us.

When we spend more time in self-battle, we realize that most of our external wars become rapidly minor. Transparency isn't for others to see us as much as it is the prism through which we see the world. Transparency adjusts our vision about who we are, and it helps to remove distractions so that we can see our place and true calling in this world.

Battle with the intent to promote growth. Fight for clarity. Commit to taking new ground, daily. Until this has been addressed the best you have to offer can never be discovered.

> **Positive Affirmation:**
> **When we spend more time in self-battle we realize that most of our external wars become rapidly minor.**

Self-Assessment Questions:

- Self-Assessment Questions:
- How do you view yourself?
- What would you say are your best qualities?
- What are some areas where you struggle?
- What would other say about your character?
- How much weight do you give to others opinion?
- Is it ever possible to measure up to everyone's opinion?
- How honest are you with yourself?
- How can being transparent to oneself can this serve with how you navigate life?
- What does it mean to you when you think of going to way with yourself?

Branded and Bold Quotes:

- "You have got to win in your mind before you win in your life."
- "Rise above the storm, and you will find the sunshine."
- "If there is no enemy within, the enemy outside can do you no harm."

- "A negative mind will never give you a positive life."
- "The greatest prison people live in, is the fear of what other people think."
- "The difference between the impossible and possible is based on a person's determination."
- "Never let a stumble in the road be the end of the journey."
- "Emotion can be the enemy; if you give into your emotion, you lose yourself. You must be at one with your emotion because the body always follows the mind." – Bruce Lee
- "All that we are is the result of what we have thought. The mind is everything. What we think, we become."
- "Don't give up. Normally it is the last key on the ring which opens the door," – Paulo Coelho

> **Action Steps:**
> **Take 20 minutes and write down things you think you have been delusional or lying to yourself about and fight for pure honesty.**

DAY 34 – READY THE RESOURCES

Where is your raw, get down and dirty attitude. There are obstacles ahead of you. You have thought about strategies. You have sized up the opposition. But it all comes down to this: With all the knowledge that you possess and things you have questioned, when are you going to shut your mouth and take action?!?! There is one thing to have the tools necessary to get the job done and another thing to step up and do it. I know it is going to be hard. It scares you so bad that you want to jump out of y our own skin. But you are going to have to tap into the ultimate resource of all, courage! Raw, no excuse, in your face, get-up and get the job done, COURAGE! Courage comes in all shape and sizes. It could be taking a stance against atrocities that impact humanity. It could be stepping in harm's way for someone who is in danger. Courage could be standing up and giving a speech that is required of you in order to pass a class. Resourcefulness is choosing to use a dose of courage to get things done. Kill the excuses. We get too comfortable chattering and talking about what we are going to do or what we going to accomplish. Shut up and start delivering! Show the world and show-up. Today is your opportunity. This is your party, prepared by time in advance for your arrival. You were given the inspiration to see what you were going to do with it. Show up for your own party.

So what if someone wants you to fail? So what if someone wants to block your way. So what, if it is hard. So what that you were born in less than ideal circumstances. The sad song sounds like a broken record. Push the needle. There is more to the song. Let it play out. It's time to dig in deep and quiet the chatter. It's time to declare your intent. But don't waist too much time talking about what you are going to do. Just go do it. Your success is ordained. It came in the form of a vision. Understand that with that vision there is natural opposition. Not to destroy you, but to develop you and make you fit for arrival. Your oppositions will shape you. So, your ultimate resources are not your tools, but simply your willingness to move. Everything you are supposed to have and experience will reveal itself. Are you ready to take that first step?

Positive Affirmation:
Everything you are supposed to have and experience will reveal itself.

Self-Assessment Questions:
- How important is courage to you?
- How do you condition your courage?

- How are you accustomed to sizing obstacles that get in your way?
- Before you tackle a touch task, do you find yourself practicing excuses for when you fail?
- Do you practice pre-failing (The speech you will give for not completing a task)?
- Before you begin a task, do you practice your victory speech?
- What weight do you give to other opinions that really want you to fail?
- What is a good use of those opinions that demand that you fail?
- How resourceful are you and gathering resources?
- What are you ultimate resources?

Branded and Bold Quotes:

- "Well, when it comes down to me against a situation, I don't like the situation to win." – MacGyver
- "You'll turn out ordinary if you're not careful." – Ann Brashares
- "Set high goals and standards for yourself; resist the temptation of the comfort zone."
- "Never give up on a dream just because of the time it will take to accomplish it. The time will pass anyway." – Earl Nightingale

- ➢ "You can only get better when you do. Do something every day to improve your key skill areas." – Brian Tracy
- ➢ "Don't be afraid to fail. Be afraid not to try."
- ➢ "If there is no struggle, there is no progress." – Frederick Douglass
- ➢ "Success is not about your resources. It's about how resourceful you are with what you have." – Tony Robbins
- ➢ "It is in your moments of decision that your destiny is shaped." – Tony Robbins
- ➢ "The difference between the impossible and possible lies in a person's determination." – Tommy Lasorda

---

Action Steps:
Make a list of resources that have aided you in the past. Describe how you can use them to aid you on your next task.

DAY 35 – GROUNDED

So you feel a little weight on your shoulders. It feels like a lot of pressure. You've never had this much weight place on you before. How did it get there? Is it there because you chose to try? To be honest, the weight would have been there weather stood still or tried. So what are you going to do with it? My suggestion is for you to fix your foundation. If you know where you stand, then you can adjust how you carry things and can shift for a better balance. You are going to try some things and fail. You're going to get creative and look for new and better ways to get things done. But if you want to get really grounded, stop for a minute, and instead of trying everything under the sun, try doing that which you really need to do. Pair down and focus.

How passionate are you about succeeding? Did you weight out the journey you must travel? Fret not. I can tell you now, that it will not be easy, but you will get better if you keep at it. This is a foundational truth. The game goes to the determined. This journey you are on is no mere journey. It is the very things that your soul needs in order to come alive. Most of us lay dormant, longing and waiting for something great to happen. However, life's not like that. To live life, you must take action. What has been encouraging you all along is a mind shift. I am asking, NO, I'm telling you to challenge your beliefs. Review what you do. If you don't check your foundation, you may be standing on something that will not sustain you, and you may be standing on something simply because you inherited it. Some of the foundations that you have been standing on may be quicksand, where the only acceptable option is to fail. But why? Why accept that when there are other presented alternatives? Is it that it goes against your initial beliefs? Any belief, worth its weight in salt or the ink it took to put it to paper deserves the right to be challenged and put to the test of fire, to see if can sustain. After all, you are banking your life on this, in many cases.

    If you know where you stand and your footing is sure, it makes it easier for you to listen your head and fix your gaze upon anything you desire. You may question if it is OK to have a desire. Someone may have told you that it is wrong to want or to have so much or more. So, before you take it as gospel, think though. Where did the person, telling that it was wrong to have more, get their philosophy, and why do they still hold to it? Do you see how it's working for them? I can say for certain, if you are living to your full potential and have acquired knowledge as well as various forms of success, one thing will move you as you experience the abundance. You will be moved not to hoard, but you will be challenged to give. The things that we have in this world today came from those that acquired and gave of themselves. So, check your foundation. Hope its solid.

> **Positive Affirmation:**
> **What you stand on determines how well you can move.**

Self-Assessment Questions:
- What responsibilities rest upon you?
- Who do you feel accountable to? Why?
- Is this obligation serving your greater good?
- Have you considered what your greater good is?
- When making a tough decision what factors do you consider?
- How do you use your failures to help you succeed?
- Do you challenge yourself toward success and in what you believe success to be?
- How do you honor your heritage?
- How do your heritage honor and support you?

Branded and Bold Quotes:

- "It's not the load that breaks you down. It's the way you carry it." – C.S. Lewis
- "Innovation is not about saying yes to everything. It's about saying no to all but the most crucial features." – Steve Jobs
- "I survived because the fire inside me burned brighter than the fire around me."

- "Stop chasing what your mind wants, and you'll get what your soul needs."
- "You can have anything you want if you are willing to give up the belief that you can't have it."
- "Struggles are required in order to survive in life because in order to stand up, you gotta know what falling down is like."
- "Mirror Mirror on the wall, I'll always get up after I fall. And whether I run, walk or have to crawl, I'll set my goals and achieve them all."
- "Growth is painful. Change is painful. But nothing is as painful as staying stuck somewhere you don't belong." – Mandy Hale
- "One reason people resist change is because they focus on what they have to give up. Instead of what they have to gain." – Rick Godwin
- "A little progress each day adds up to big results."

> **Action Steps:**
> **Sit down with someone you respect and ask questions about where they got their governing heritage and why they practice it. Seek the value.**

WEEK 6 – GO!

Bold Declaration #6 - <u>GO:</u> I will **GO** and set this world on fire with my unlimited being and transform its future.

Things we have in this world came from visionaries who had a desire to move things from their head into reality. They shaped this world by their thoughts. They did a lot of trials and had a lot of errors, and they didn't let failures defined them, but they used every failure to build something great. Action and motion drove them. They failed forward. Knowing that as long as they keep trying that they would eventually succeed.

The civilized world came through a lot of trial by fire. Men and women who wanted better and believed hard enough that they willed the change. They defied customs and traditions and were determined to make things better. That is at the core of every human. It's a seed that has been planted in all of our DNA. However, it takes the right level of events to nurture it. Some of our growth come through a great deal of pressure. What we produce comes from perseverance.

It takes guts to go against the grain. Seeing things that are going one way and practiced by a mass of people, then to introduce things that seem illogical, but because you held to your belief, introduced something that ultimately made life better. You must be willing to be burned up upon the fires of tradition in order to get to something better. It can be done with respect, but you have to know your vision, and you have to be willing to communicate what you believe, even when others are trying to quiet you down. If you are passionate about introducing something for the betterment of humanity, then eventually you will find the right ear that will listen, and you may even get others to come alongside you to aid you in your passion. Stay true and never give up on you.

You will go through some tough trial in order to arrive. You will be conditioned on the journey. You will have your eyes opened to new possibilities as you preserver. Give thanks for being chosen to have this vision and stay in an attitude of the excitement of the possibilities. But if you really want to set this world on fire, duplicate yourself.

You see, traditionally, in order for a mentor, mentee relationship to develop, it takes the passion of a mentee to seek out a mentor, then the work begins. However, I say, if you want really do some serious shaping of the next 20 years for what will happen in this world, then go on the offence. You are in the home stretch of this training. You are about to blow the lid off of your life and future. Why not get serious and deliberate and go and share this with others. Seek out someone who could benefit from this journey. Take time to get another copy of this book **(If you have signed up for the mailing list and have indicated that you have completed this book at AmericanGoGetter.com/BrandedandBold Select, "I want to be a mentor" and get a 20% off coupon.).** Find another individual, not just to give the book too, but commit to spending the next six week, working with and walking them through the thought process.

This action along will produce people who will be in tune with themselves and are bold enough to go and shape the makeup of this worlds future.

Are you ready to GO! Let's go do it!

DAY 36 - A TRAVELED ROAD

The road you have been on has been loaded with challenges up until now. You have learned some inspirational things along the way. In our journey over the weeks, I am sure you have been made aware of and have come in contact with some people that have given you spark and their stories have encouraged hope. They have made the impossible seem more real and tangible.

You have witnessed the stories of triumph, hope, and perseverance. Wow! These stories have stretched you. Moved your mind to a new level. Your eyes are opened wide. No longer do you interpret struggles and trials as means to stop or defeat you. You see them as stepping stones. Opportunities for a challenge to move you to the next level of life. What a gift it is to take a backhanded insult and turn it into pure motivation. What an encouragement to be moved from an attitude of defeat, into an attitude of unrelenting fire.

The road you are on still had a covering and blinders on as to how you will get there, but as for now, you know that it's all about faith. The kind of faith that grows like a seed. A faith that lets you know that the things you hope for are out there. Calling, waiting in the dark. Your treasure awaits in the great abyss. You can't rest. You have to keep moving toward that call. For you know that its calling is tied to your identity. Not the identity that you were called by others, but the identity that waits for you at the final destiny. In reality, as you travel the road, you pick up pieces of that identity. Bit by bit, you collect habits, traits, and trends that move you into becoming the person you were destined to be, based on the goal you are pursuing.

The goal is not the goal. The goal is simply the thing that got you on the road. As you travel, you will start to see that it was the willingness to get on the road is the very thing that you were after all along.

So, pay attention. Look at who's on that road with you. Pay attention to their attitude and habits. Look at those that have reached their stated goals. What are you learning from them? Check out the scenery along your path. Is it any different than when you first started? Does it inspire you? Are things getting brighter? How do you view your placement and your calling? Do you find yourself challenged in every way? Do you find it fulfilling? What about the people you are called to serve? How are you impacting their lives? Are their lives any better because you showed up?

Those are some deep question, so are you ready to travel? Are you ready to give an answer?

Don't stop! Get up! I know it hurts! Keep moving! The change is about to happen! The transformation you need to experience is about to happen. It awaits you right after that last step you thought you could not take. So, press harder. Go for it. Dig deep. Save the rest time for later. Your breakthrough is about to happen. You are about to learn something today. Keep your eyes on the prize. Make a believer out of yourself as well as your nay-sayers. Develop a faith that is tested through is trial of fire. Become undeniable.

> **Positive Affirmation:**
> **Your goals are not the goals. They only get you on the road and get you moving. That was the original goal.**

Self-Assessment Questions:

- Do you know where the road you're on is taking you?
- Do you have a choice about your road selection?
- Whose life-path have you been observing has inspired you?
- What habit characteristic have you observed in their practice?
- What obstacles have you observed that are in your path?
- What resources have you gathered in order to combat these obstacles?
- What new habit traits have you observed that you have put into practice? How are they working for you?
- Do you understand the benefit of these new traits?
- Do you feel motivated and confident about reaching your goals, more so than when you started this book?

Branded and Bold Quotes:

- Take action! An inch of movement will bring you closer to your goals than a mile of intention." – Dr. Steve Maraboli
- "Success is liking yourself, liking what you do, and liking how you do it." – Maya Angelo
- "Success is going from failure to failure without losing your enthusiasm." – Winston Churchill
- "An object at rest will tend to remain at rest. An object that is in motion will tend to remain in motion." – Issac Newton
- "You only fail when you stop trying."
- 'Success is a journey, not a destination. The doing is often more important than the outcome." – Arthur Ashe
- "Be committed to the process without being emotionally attached to the results."
- "It is better to take many small steps in the right direction than to make a great leap forward only to stumble backward." – Proverb
- By recording your dreams and goals on paper, you set in motion the process of becoming the person you most want to be. Put your future in good hands – your own." – Mark Victor Hansen
- "I'm on the hunt for who I've not yet become."

> **Action Steps:**
> **Take a moment to measure who and how you were 5 weeks ago. What are the notable differences? List them.**

DAY 37 - SOUL ON FIRE

The image of fire conjures emotions of heat. When there is flame, it can bring warmth on a cold day. But what happens when you get too close to the flame? If you've been burnt before, you quickly go to hard lessons learned. You had a pain limitation set in. You taught yourself to live in the moment, versus thriving into eternity. You see, if you look at pain or anything that causes fear in light of time, it loses its bite. Pain and fire are limited to small moments. But to a mind that is tuned for eternity, it then right sizes fear. It takes and hones the fire. Instead of letting the flames on the outside shape and limit, an eternally minded warrior fire burns from within. They use that fire to shape and form their destiny. They go into hot pursuit. Their beliefs move them. They don't make childhood wishes and dreams. They work! They work hard and press through the fires and limitations that are in front of them.

Darkness tries to consume them, but the fire that is within burns and illuminates to brighten as it cuts through the lies of the past and brightens the future. Their fire burns so bright that it brings inspiration. It inspires hope. A person on fire is a seed planter. They know that every action they take today is always about investing in a brighter tomorrow. They know the score, but they don't dwell on the scoreboard. Not in the middle of the game. It's all about how things are going to end up. It takes a continuous victories attitude to produce a win. There are too many oppositions out there too passive in its approach. It takes a fire. It takes pressure to build. It takes a little guy to stand face to face with their own personal giant. Mainly to win, all it takes is it to stand. Yes, you will get knocked down, but the key is to keep standing. Don't give into the lie. The finest steel has to go through the hottest fire. Will you withstand the trial of fire? Will you show the world what you are made of? Not the limited flesh and blood or broken bones? You are so much more than this minor limitations. Your fires burn deep and are fueled by your anchored faith.

Allow yourself to become passionate. Get tuned in and turned up about the thing you are going after. That calling placed upon you for a reason. The journey you are on is going to shape you. Step-by-step. Trial-by-trial. It's; all about shaping you. It's moving you into becoming a person of action. Will you rise? Will you break the chains that are holding you? GO for it. Get after your destiny. Pick up speed. Chase it down till you find it. Server notice to your future. You are coming, holding a torch and ready to set your world on fire.

Positive Affirmation:
Don't fear the flame. Be the flame

Self-Assessment Questions:

- What are you known fears?
- How often do you think about them?
- The things that you fear has anything every defeated them before?
- In a comparison of a moment to eternity how big, really, are the things that you fear?
- Are you fearful or excited about the future?
- What things are you inspired to go out and shape in the near future?
- How confident are you with your ability to shape the future?
- What resources do you need to influence your confidence?

Branded and Bold Quotes:

- "Be fearless in the pursuit of what sets your soul on fire."
- "You get what you work for not what you wish for."
- "The darkest night produces the brightest stars."
- "Let your light shine so bright that others can see their way out of the dark."
- "Your future is created by what you do today, not tomorrow."
- "The finest steel has to go through the hottest fire." – Richard M. Nixon
- "All things splendid have been achieved by those who dared believe that something inside them was superior to circumstance…" – Bruce Barion
- "Passion is energy. Feel the power that comes from focusing on what excites you." – Oprah Winfrey

- "Success seems to be connected with action. Successful people keep moving. They make mistakes, but they don't quit." – Conrad Hilton
- "Gratitude unlocks the fullness of life."

> **Action Steps:**
> **Review your goals with a friend and set dates to when you will put them to action.**

DAY 38 - CLIMB!

To run a marathon, you can't start a race with the expectation that within a single step to complete the race. To swim any length of an ocean, you can't start and expect to swim the full distance in a single stroke. In order to climb a mountain, you can expect to reach the top within a single step up. It takes hard work, training, and repetition. Success requires to you to condition your body to respond to the challenges. It requires an enormous amount of focus. Interwoven in that is a hefty dose of courage. The common temptation is to quite.

This is way too hard. This could kill you. Is this worth it? Why are doing this? This is a short list of the internal chatter of which we commonly get from others. But still, you must climb. Fix your focus on what you came to do. You have personal reasons why you must climb. Whatever it may be, you will die inside each day you choose not to engage. Don't allow yourself to stop till you get to the top. For at the top is where you will find total self-discovery.

At the top is where you will find how powerful you really are. You're going to find that this mountain was no more powerful than the thoughts and limitations in your mind. The world's toughest mountains have been flattened. The selective mountains in your life have been conquered by someone else already. Let that sink in. The reason that most people fail is that they choose to subscribe to the stories that rumor that they can't. Throw away that magazine. Change the channel. Seek a new source. Let the new truth drive deep down inside of you. Let the desire to succeed burn deep inside you. Use that fuel to take one massive step, one right after the other.

Today is the day you stop the lies. You move obstacles out of your way. Today you take action. Become relentless. You will ascend that mountain. One grueling step at a time, but with an un-surrendered will. You will make it or die trying. There is no other option. Commit today to change your vantage point. That mountain will show you things about yourself. It will draw greatness out of you and make it rise to the surface. The mountain is not there to break you as it is there to shape you.

The mountain is your classroom. It is your testing ground. The mountain is the doorway that leads you to the next demotion. To put it deeper, each step you take up that mountain is a series of doorways. Each step opens more and more doors. Each step inspires hope. Each steps chips and reshapes who you are. It invokes and brings forth your called identity. The mountain is a gift. So, are you going to climb or just sit there and think about? No! Get climbing. Don't stop!

Positive Affirmation:
The mountain is your classroom

Self-Assessment Questions:

- What are your normal expectations about winning?
- What does it take for you to experience a win or a victory?
- Describe emotionally what it feels like to win?
- Describe what it feels like to lose?
- How does all of that emotion go into your preparation for the task that is in front of you?
- Do you view life as hard or challenging? (The words you choose matter)
- Describe the people in your immediate circle. Do most of them support our hinder your drive to succeed?
- How important is it to you to have positive reinforcements on the challenging task that you must face?
- How does it encourage you to know that the task that you are about to tackle has already been conquered by someone else? (There's no competition. Just role models)
- What have you learned about yourself when it comes to how you face challenges?

Branded and Bold Quotes:

- "Opportunities to find deeper powers within ourselves come when life seems most challenging," – Joseph Campbell

- "Set your goals high and don't stop till you get there." – Bo Jackson
- "Look for the opportunities in the difficulties, not the difficulties in the opportunities."
- "The person who says it cannot be done should not interrupt the person who is doing it." – Chinese Proverb
- "It's not the mountain we conquer, but ourselves." – Sir Edmund Hillary
- "You can't fall if you don't climb. But there's no joy in living your whole life on the ground." – Unknown
- "You must climb before you can enjoy the view."
- "Every mountain top is within reach if you just keep climbing." – Barry Friday
- "Climb mountains, not so the world can see you, but so you can see the world."
- "The question isn't who is going to let me; but who is going to stop me."

**Action Steps:
Tackle 3 significant things that are on your goal list today. Don't think. Just do it!**

DAY 39 - REACH!

This is the day it gets real! You wanted to move forward. Well, I gotta tell you, it comes with pain. The kind of pain that will break you down. It will make you want to cry out. You will take action today that will tax your mind and body. But you gotta get set in your mind this key phrase, "Just one more..." One more rep. One more call to a client. One more door to knock on. One more chapter to read. One more item to assemble. Inconvenient. Painful. But so worth it. But choosing to press in and do one more, it will be the catalyst that will make all the difference. That one more will turn this impossible thing into an all of a sudden moment.

That's that moment where it seems to the rest of the world that you came out of nowhere with a ton of success. They will not see the hard work you put in. They will not see the tears or the sweat. They will not hear the heartbreaking of the insults from the nay-sayers. But they will see you. They will witness your arrival. But that won't come until you commit to them, "Just one more," attitude.

Make the decision to be different. Continually transform from what you were yesterday, and into what you were called to be.

There are people waiting for the transformation you to arrive. The world is sick and hemorrhaging. You are the cure. You are the medicine they have been waiting on. Bring the hope. Just one more. It's time to set all excuses aside. It's time to arrive. Every day, show up. Put in. Press, build and grow. Transform. Don't show up tomorrow as your weaker self. It does the world no good. The world needs you to shine. The world needs you to past the test of the fire. The world needs its champion.

Don't be afraid to dream and never sell yourself short in that you can't grow into that dream. When it comes to the power of the mind, there is no limit. Your mind can quickly take you to your lowest hell and just as quick, shoot you through the stratosphere. So, will you let your mind soar? Stretch out your wings. Flap one more time. Yes, there is resistance, but all it takes is a will to flap. One more time and one more time after that. Speak to your future and claim your calling. It's right there. Waiting on you. Dig in one good time. Reach!

Positive Affirmation:
Every day, let the best you show up!

Self-Assessment Questions:
- Describe a painful moment or trial you recently went through?
- How did it feel to fail or give up?
- Were there any regrets?
- Before your body quit, did you quit in your own head?

- Where you able to visualize how it felt to give up or quit?
- In moments where you succeeded, did you visualize how it would feel to complete something?
- Did it feel as good once you completed it as it did in your mind?
- Have you measured your breaking point? What would it take for you to go one more layer past that point?
- How important is it to you to transform? Are you expecting anything on the other side?
- Your mind has teased you with the possibilities. So are you willfully pursuing the thing that you have dreamed about?
- Are you seeing signs of confirmation that you are on the right path?

Branded and Bold Quotes:

- "The pain you feel today is the strength you feel tomorrow. For every challenge encountered is an opportunity for growth." – Unknown
- "When obstacles arise, you change your direction to reach your goal; you do not change your decision to get there." – Zig Ziglar
- "There are two options: Make progress or make excuses."
- "Growing is painful. Change is painful. But nothing is as painful as staying stuck somewhere you don't belong."
- "Don't make excuses! Make changes! - Tony Gaskins

- "Don't wait until you reach your goal to be proud of yourself. Be proud of each step you take toward reaching that goal."
- "The road to character is built by confronting your own weakness."
- "You should set goals beyond your reach, so you always have something to live for." – Ted Turner
- There is no passion to be found in playing small – In settling for a life that is less than the one you are capable of living." – Nelson Mandela
- "Be stubborn about your goals, and flexible about your methods."

> **Action Steps:**
> **Pick one of your goals where you have hit the breaking point. Try again, TODAY, and see if you can shatter that limitation.**

DAY 40 - GROW!

Like a seed planted in the ground, its purpose and intent are to grow. It responds to nurturing and nutrients. If fed it will grow. Depending on the type of seed, it may have to grow through some fierce opposition in order to produce what it was designed to deliver. It may have to endure growing under some of the harshest conditions; Soil that may be weak in nutrients. A lack of water or even too much water. An extreme blast from the sun. But, a seed that is placed under intention has all the needed parameters to grow to success. It may take some time, but with work and determination, it shall produce.

Like the seed, we are called to grow. All of us have been placed on this earth under care and with intent. Each of us has been granted the means to experience growth and produce. What some lack is the knowledge that we are seeds with purpose. We will face opposition, but we have mainly 2 choices. To grow or to just exist. But for certain, growth will not come from comfort. So it's time to get comfortable with being uncomfortable. Become so familiar with it until the uncomfortable becomes easy. That is the moment you know you're experiencing growth.

The hardest place that we have to experience discomfort is in our mind. This is the ultimate battleground. When we willfully do batter here, then any battle that we have to experience externally has to fold when facing who we are becoming. The battles in our minds refine us. It enables us to be prepared for the next level of life. It keeps the main thing as the main thing.

When we grow, we get to refine the identity and image that we were called into being. When we were called, that was a lax and minor state of being. We were worthy to be called, but a calling means we have to move from the place of origin to the destination. As we move from point A to point B, that is where our true identity is formed. The journey is designed with things that will cause pain. It has traps and snares. They were placed there intentionally. Not to kill you but to train and sharpen you. For where you arrive, will require a person who is capable of defending their position. Your trials are the very thing that will give you the skills you need to not only arrive but to hold and fully occupy your destiny.

There is a temptation to get to a destination and to take comfort in knowing you arrived, then to sit back and kick-up your heels and feel good that you don't have to do anything else. However, if you have been paying attention to the growth process, you will then start to see, that growth is a part of a series and is not a destination, but a lifestyle. To grow on a regular basis moves you to a state of fulfillment. It takes on an addictive-like quality, which is non-detrimental but extremely supportive of a balanced life. Life should never be treated as something that you get older in and at a certain point, you decide that you are old then you lay down and rest and give up. No, you keep growing because it is part of our human DNA that we have been conditioned to deny.

So, once again. Get in the mirror and get all up in your own face. Decide that you are going to grow every day and in every way. You are not going to give up, give in, or sit back and wait for death to come get you. If death wants you, death is going to have to search really hard to find you, and once it finds you, it will find you doing. Leaving nothing in the tank, but truly dying on E.

> **Positive Affirmation:**
> **Growth will not come from comfort.**

Self-Assessment Questions:

- What areas of your life have you experienced growth?
- What are some contributing factors that lead to your growth?
- What are your areas where you have hit roadblocks?
- What resources do you need to break through your growth roadblocks?
- Is it OK if instead of growing, you simply maintain?
- How is that satisfying to your soul?
- Do you ever go to war with yourself?
- Does it bother you to know that there are moments where there are supposed to be some pain?
- How do you use pain to your advantage?

Branded and Bold Quotes:

- "In any given moment we have two options: To step forward into growth or to step back into safety." – Abraham Maslow
- "Great things never come from comfort zones."
- "Success is never owned, it's rented. And rent is due every day."
- "I do not fix my problems. I fix my thinking. Then problems fix themselves." – Louise L. Hay
- "It takes courage to grow up and become who you really are." – E. E. Cummings
- "When a flower doesn't bloom you fix the environment in which it grows, not the flower." – Alexander Den Heijer
- "Something will grow from all you are going through. And it will be you." – Toby Mac
- "If we're growing, we're always going to be out of our comfort zone." – John Maxwell
- "Strength and growth come only through continuous effort and struggle…"
- "Your mind is a garden. Your thoughts are seeds. You can grow flowers, or you can grow weeds."
- "Courage is never to let your fears influence your actions." – Arthur Koestler
- "Everyone can rise above their circumstances and achieve success if they are dedicated to and passionate about what they do."

> **Action Steps:**
> Go out and take a brisk walk or do an activity that charges your mind and reflect on your next task.

DAY 41 - REACH FOR THE HEAVENS

What is your limitation? Who gave it to you? Who convinced you that you had limits? Was it given to you but someone else who was scared and choosing to live to a limit that was handed to them? Take some time to get real and personal. I am challenging you to think. I mean think deep. What happens to the really big dreamers?

Back in the 60's, there was a thing called the Great Space Race. America, led by John F. Kennedy made a commitment that we will put a man on the moon. This was something never done before. But the inspiration was there. People believed. This commitment rallied the best to step forward in order to make this far off dream a reality. Some said it was foolish to shoot for the stars. They said it could not be done. But there is something about when you have a belief that is locked on and set on a sight that's beyond what you can see or to a place where you have never been.

Hope moves people. Hope inspires the masses. Even where it is presented as a frail underdog. The challenge is being given now. It's time to get up and go toe-to-toe with life. It is time to get in the ring with your giants. You are going to need to bring your biggest belief. Set your sights high and keep reaching higher. The higher you go, the more you inspire. You see, any effort you put in to transform your life, inspires others to do the same.

Grow into your goals. When you started, it was as if a little kid has put on his dads pants and shirt and couldn't quite fill them out. But day-by-day, the child had a role model to pursue and a fire burning inside. They didn't quite know it at the time, but they had a destiny they were to fulfill. The fantasizing while filling their fathers' clothes was the spark and reminder of what could be.

So what! It's going to be hard to. You didn't get the best start. You didn't come from the best family. You were not born with the right skin color or were not born with the right contentment. Good points, but very weak excuses. What does any of that have to do with where your focus should be? When you look up in the sky, we all have the same vantage point. The SKY! It calls to all of us and says to each of us, Yes you can! Don't create barriers that were not there, to begin with.

Use your imagination. I mean get really playful with it. Dream of anything and everything. Dream of cures for cancer. Dream of flying cars. Dream of cities under the sea. Dream of unlimited travel to anywhere in the universe. What your mind can conceive, your work, commitment, and effort can achieve. Let your mind run free. It is not a childish teaser. It is a gift from the creator and is the playground where He meets you to play and plan your future. Don't forsake that interaction. Dream big and shoot for the stars. Heaven awaits.

> **Positive Affirmation:**
> **Don't just dream for the stars. Dream beyond.**

Self-Assessment Questions:

- How did you come to know that you had a limitation?
- How did you come to believe in that limitation?
- What confirmed your limitation?
- Did you test the truths of the limitations?
- When you learned that the limitation was not as real as what was initially stated, how did that make you feel?
- What desire beyond the stars did you give up on? Does that desire still call to you?
- How does it make you feel when you haven't moved toward your desire?
- What will it take to get you to move?
- What excuses or stories have you rehearsed that describe or support your reasons for not pursuing your goals?
- How playful are you with your dreams?

Branded and Bold Quotes:

> "Study not what the world is doing, but what you can do for it."

- "Set a goal so big you can't achieve it until you grow into the person who can."
- "It is not in the stars to hold our destiny but in ourselves." – William Shakespeare
- "The future belongs to those who believe in the beauty of their dreams." – Eleanor Roosevelt
- "Don't miss out on something that could be amazing, just because it could also be difficult."
- "Every great dream begins with a dreamer. Always remember, you have within you the strength, the patience, and the passion to reach for the stars to change the world." – Harrett Tubman
- "Keep your eyes on the stars, and your feet on the ground." – Theodore Roosevelt
- "Men are not prisoners of fate, but only prisoners of their own minds." – Franklin D. Roosevelt
- "I have loved the stars too fondly to be fearful of the night."
- "Sometimes unforeseen opportunities emerge from the remnants of life's challenges… Sometimes it is possible to transform tough times into great growth and success." – Kay Douglas

---

Action Steps:
Think of the craziest and outlandish thing that you want to accomplish. Write it down and

DAY 42 - LIFT UP!

How bright is your light? Does it twinkle like a tiny little Christmas lights or does it beam bright into the eyes of others and blind them? Both are lights yet extreme in contrast. In a dark room, a single little light has the power to illuminate and even calm fears where they were once terror. Light can be used to light the path and lead the way. It is all in the application. In the bigger scheme of things, it is not as important how bright your light is, as it is to understand how your light is being applied. Do you know who your light is inspiring? Not only does your light bring sight, but are you letting your light emotionally warm someone's spirit? You have been granted that power and that responsibility.

As you arise and grow and engage life at its highest level, there are those that are watching you. They are wanting to know your story. They see the results you are getting, but they not only need to see the finished product, but they need to know what's under the hood. They need to know the blood and guts and nitty-gritty of your story. They needed to know what inspired you and pulled you along the path. They need to know what held you on the path when you wanted to give up countless times. They need to know about the sleepless nights and the hard work and long hours you put in. They need to know about the sacrifices you made. They need to know about the loved ones that support you along the journey and the ones that you support and serve and the motivation to keep you climbing.

As you walk this journey and are blessed by this experience, understand that you were also set aflame like a torch for others to see. People come from miles around to see a good fire. So burn and burn brightly. Be a force to transform people's vision. Always leave people better than when you first found them. Tell your awesome story. Captivate the minds of others and take them on a journey that leads back to their own. Inspire them to live, write and make their own story. Show them that they each have a treasure inside and they have to do some digging to find it. Dig it up and bring it to the surface. What good is a treasure if it is not used?

Commit to taking others on your journey. There is an air of darkness that exists in all of our lives. You have to take a journey to learn how to turn the lights on. Now it's your time to light up the world. We can either continue to be a part of the problem, or we can step up and be the solution. Look around. There is someone who was just like you. Don't let them flop around and gasp for air like you did. Go to them and be deliberate and invest your time in moving them to the next level. Do something so bold that when you die the preacher will not have to lie and make up stuff about you. But let the lives that you touched be your living testimony.

> **Positive Affirmation:**
> We can either continue to be a part of the problem, or we can step up and be the solution.

Self-Assessment Questions:

- In what ways do you bring illumination and enlightenment to your environment?
- Are you stratified with how things are in this world?
- Where do you best classify yourself? An observer of life or an agent of change?
- Who are the people that admire and look up to you?
- Who are the people that regularly seek your advice?
- Have you taken time to not only give the solution but to explain to them how you got to the solution of life?
- If you were to spend the next 6 months mentoring a group of people, what might you hope to see develop in them?
- Do you have 30 minutes to an hour, one a week, to meet with and work with mentoring another individual?

Branded and Bold Quotes:

- "I want to inspire people. I want someone to look at me and say because of you; I didn't give up."
- "We rise by lifting others."
- "Don't be ashamed of your story. It will inspire others."
- "Having influence is not about elevating self, but about lifting others. – Sheri Dew
- "Be a rainbow in someone else's cloud."
- "I cannot teach anybody anything. I can only make them think." – Socrates
- "The key is, no matter what story you tell. Make your buyer the hero." – Chris Brogan
- "The greatest good you can do for another is not just to share your riches but to reveal to him his own." – Benjamin Disraeli
- "In learning, you will teach, and in teaching, you will learn." – Phil Collins
- "We all need someone who inspires us to do better than we know how."

Action Steps:
Pick someone to mentor. Order them a book. Ask them could you spend the next 6 weeks mentoring them.

CONCLUSION

Whew! That was a lot to think about and chew on. I was referring to myself. It was a powerful journey I have been on, and it was even more powerful to go back through my journals and see the things that I learned and engrained in my thinking. As I was writing much of this, I allowed myself to fast forward the clock. To the time where I would be a really old man. I was contemplating the things I would think about at that time. I would naturally think about the aches and pain left by the battle scars of life, but along with that, I thought about regret. The things I left unfinished. The places I wanted to visit, but never did. The people that I wanted to express love and thanks to, but never had a chance. That thought served as motivation to get this book done. I have had so many regrets up until now, but this book is not one of them.

I love you all. I genuinely love you all. You took the time to take this journey with me. You crawled up inside my mind. It was cold, dark and damp in places. I hope it didn't scare you too much. In other parts, you saw signs of renovation. Yes, great things are happening. I am so glad I came up with enough courage to get this out of me and on to paper. It was a painful stretch, but so worth it.

Along with this journey, you learned how to ask some really good and deep questions. You learned how to empower yourself by asking questions that move you instead of crippling your progress. In section 1 you learned how to **DREAMS** and the importance of it. Dreaming keeps the mind fertile, and it expands the possibilities. It helps you to connect with your calling and get you sparked about discovering your own identity.

In **section 2**, you got to **WAKE UP** to what is going on around you. Seeing that there is so much more. You learned how to recognize when and where others are managing your life and destiny and that you could get more out of life if you simply choose to manage your own.

In **section 3**, you started to **ARISE**. You moved from your complacent place of rest and made the conscious decision to get on the road of life. Here, you gain the understanding that no one else is going to live your life for you. Life is to be lived and to its fullest degree. It is to be lived by you. But it won't be lived you are still lying in the bed.

In **section 4**. This is where you got serious about getting things in motion. Here is where you got centered on what you are supposed to be doing. Ridding yourself of all other things that are not related to your calling, and acquiring help and connection that will enable you to see success. Like a runner taking the starting blocks, you are down and in position. **READY** to explode off the track and show the world what you are made of.

Section 5 – This is where you get locked in and **SET**. The race is enviable. You are ready to set the world on fire with the breakneck speed in which you will move. You are setting yourself up to jump in and manage your world. Fulfilling your purpose and calling.

Section 6- Here is where you explode. BOOM! **GO!** Here is where you get things done. Move all obstacles out of the way. Jumping over barriers. Digging in deep and discover who you are. Pushing your mind, body, and spirit to its fulfilled calling.

In the last part of section 6, I eluded to mentoring. This is something that I am very big on. When I was growing up, I wanted to start my own business, and I was advised to get a mentor. At that point, I ignored that advice and mad a disaster of my original business venture. After years of mature, I am a huge proponent of mentoring. But I am more intentional about it these days. I seek out mentors all the time. It saves me time and headaches. But the next level is where I am very intentional about seeking out people I could potentially mentor. That was the birth of this book. And I want to take it to the next level here.

How would like to be responsible for transforming our culture? I would like to challenge each of you to assist me in that endeavor. You have just spent an intense week of opening your mind and improving your thinking and were moved to take action daily. Imagine how powerful it would be if you used this book and came alongside someone else and mentored them through this, read transformational assignment. Yes, I am proposing that you take another 6 weeks out of your life and commit to working with an individual and led them through this thought process. You don't have to check in with them each and every day, but you can get them a copy of this book and tell them how it has encouraged and moved you and that you see something in them that is worthy of some attention and guidance. Let them know that you see their potential. Use this book to not only inspire them but as a tool to build a powerful connection between you two.

Go to www.Americangogetter.com/BrandedAndBold and order them and copy of the book today. Get started on the journey. Change the world.

PROLOG

Remember the 6 bold declarations? Let me remind you once more:

<u>6 Bold Declarations:</u>

1. **DREAM**: I will accept my divine DREAM without limits and seek every way possible to move them into reality.

2. **AWAKE:** I will AWAKEN to my true calling and pursue it with relentless passion

3. **ARISE**: I will ARISE and engage life at its highest level.

4. **READY:** I will make myself READY for challenges, knows and unknown through resources I collect.

5. **SET:** I will SET my focus, plan, and commitment and will only settle for success.

6. GO: I will GO and set this world on fire with my unlimited being and transform its future.

And let's not forget the contract I made with myself:

My contract:

I will get this finished work and all of its expanded development into the hands of people around the globe and encourage them to discover their identity and calling and take ownership of shaping their destiny with a high sense of responsibility. I will encourage my readers to engage in mentorship at the heights level. I am committed to instituting a distribution platform that will get this program in the hands of 6 MILLION people within 6 years (By December 31, 2023) by any means necessary.

This is so important to me and to the makeup of the future of this world.

It was so hard to limit what I placed in this labor of love. There is so much more to say, but I had to fight to cut things out or this would have been too overwhelming and may have lost its structure of effectiveness. But rest assured, as long as I am able I will keep producing. Above all my greatest achievements nothing is more important than the phenomenal relationships I got to develop with so many people all around the globe. I am so glad you took this journey with me. I am even more excited to get to know you on a personal level. Can you do me a favor and make sure that you are on my mailing list. Go to www.americangogetter.com/mentorheroes and sign up. I want to keep you apprised of any new developments. I want you to share your story. I want to hear about your success and also if you are having any struggles that you are trying to find a breakthrough. Let me help in any way I can. If I don't have the answers, I will fight to get you in front of the most effective resources.

I have been stretched and moved into a state of belief. I have traveled and seen things that have blown my mind. I have witnessed some powerful transformations. I hope that I conveyed that effectively to you in this writings project. May it be a continuous blessing to you as you review and re-read and especially as you sit down and share your journey with others you are going to mentor. If you are serious about taking the mentor challenge, then I am serious about coming alongside you. So, if you are willing to take on 2 people to mentor over the next years, I want to get you set up as soon as possible. And because you chose to take this challenge, I want to offer a discounted special for you. In order to get the discounted coupon, go to www.americangogetter.com/mentorheroes and register, and I will send you a coupon code to get your mentor kit at a reduced price. Thanks for stepping up and letting yourself be a force powerful enough to change the trajectory of this world. Now go and live a legendary life. I'm excited to see the results and grateful to be a tool of usefulness.

Eternal Blessings To You!

Curtis L. Walker, Author

ABOUT THE AUTHOR:

Curtis Walker is a second-time author and lover and liver of life. He was born in Pontiac, Michigan and lived in Michigan for most of his life. He is married to Tamara, and they have two adult children, Jonathan and Lina. He spent nine years in the U. S. Marine Reserves from 1992 to 2003. He is a graduate of the University of Phoenix with a B. S. in Information Technology. He is the sole brother of four older sisters and very proud of it. He loves his family and encourages them daily. He is engaged in his community and world relief missions. Stay plugged in and keep your eyes open for other great books like this one to come out shortly.

www.ingramcontent.com/pod-product-compliance
Lightning Source LLC
Chambersburg PA
CBHW031642170426
43195CB00035B/367